To Sister Judith

DECIDING TO KNOW GOD IN A DEEPER WAY

Be Arrested by His Grace

SAM TITA

That which God has destined for you Must Come to Pass.

Rom 15:18

DECIDING TO **KNOW**

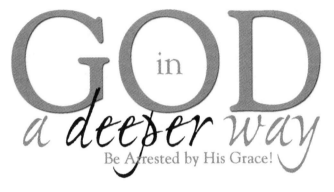

GOD in

a deeper way

Be Arrested by His Grace!

SAM TITA

Foreword by Pastor Bob Johnston

CASTLE QUAY BOOKS

Deciding to Know God in a Deeper Way : Be Arrested by His Grace!

Copyright ©2011 Sam Tita
All rights reserved
Printed in Canada
International Standard Book Number: 978-1-894860-45-1

Published by:
Castle Quay Books
1307 Wharf Street, Pickering, Ontario, L1W 1A5
Tel: (416) 573-3249
E-mail: info@castlequaybooks.com
www.castlequaybooks.com

Copy edited by Marina H. Hofman Willard
Cover design by Essence Publishing
Printed at Essence Publishing, Belleville, Ontario

Library and Archives Canada Cataloguing in Publication
Tita, Sam, 1969-
     Deciding to know God in a deeper way : be arrested by
his grace! / Sam Tita ; foreword by Bob Johnston.
ISBN 978-1-894860-45-1

     1. Grace (Theology). I. Title.
BT761.3.T58 2010   234   C2010-907832-2

CASTLE QUAY BOOKS

CONTENTS

FOREWORD

od saves us, not because of our own human efforts and what we have done, but according to His own purpose and mercy. He does it by the power of His grace.

Sam Tita is a living, powerful example of the power of God's grace. It's the power of God unto wholeness and complete restoration. You can rely on self-efforts and willpower all you want, but they can bring you only so far. It is only the power of God's amazing grace that can set you free from all bondages.

Grace is given to us by God so that we can be victorious over a life of sin. Your life can be turned around and given hope and purpose, all because of God's marvellous grace!

Grace is given so that we can serve God acceptably with reverence and godly fear. The apostle Paul writes, *"Wherefore we receiving a kingdom which cannot be moved, let us have grace, whereby we may serve God acceptably with reverence and godly fear: For our God is a consuming fire"* (Hebrews 12:28-29, KJV). We don't serve God without grace, but we serve and reverence God because of His grace. Those who allow the Grace of God to manifest in their circumstances experience major changes and go on to live lives full of testimonies.

I believe this book will touch you and transform you. It's a book, not only about "His grace," but how to appropriate His grace. Sam's desire is to help us realize how blessed and deeply loved we are by our Father in heaven.

You haven't picked up this book by accident. I believe you will find in these pages a fresh perspective regarding achieving your destiny through the power of God's grace!

Pastor Bob Johnston
Senior Pastor, Global Kingdom Ministries

ACKNOWLEDGEMENTS

No human being can exist in isolation and function meaningfully for any extended period of time. God created us to coexist, to relate and assist one another.

That has been my personal experience over the years. In fact, there are many whose relationships and assistance I no longer deserve because of my own shortcomings but who, by the Grace of God, have extended mercy and love regardless.

My dear wife, Naomi, is a shining example of that group of persons. I thank her for her tireless support, encouragement and love throughout this project and in the many endeavours of our lives.

I thank my children, Emmanuel, Belinda, Samuel and Pearl-Catherine, who have allowed me the pleasure of continuing to be their father and have not "divorced" me in spite of my innumerable mistakes earlier in their lives.

I thank my pastor, Reverend Bob Johnston, and the staff and volunteers of Global Kingdom Ministries for all their support.

I extend a very special thanks to my dear friend Vashi Sakhrani and his wife, Stella, whom God used to cause this project to materialize.

To my friends and partners Moses and Patricia Mawa and all the others too numerous to mention, thank you.

Finally, I thank my greatest mentor, teacher, encourager and guide. His name is Jesus. Why He would choose me I have no idea, but I am eternally grateful. This whole project is about Him. If you don't know Him, then I pray that you will allow Him to do for you what He's done for me and the countless others around the world who have allowed Him into their lives.

INTRODUCTION

You will probably agree with me that the difference between knowing something and not knowing it, or having specific knowledge on a particular subject and not having it, usually narrows down to a moment in time, sometimes as narrow as just a split second. Therefore in one moment you are "unaware" and in the next moment you enter into "awareness." It is as though you're standing facing a wall that has a secret door, but the door blends so perfectly with the wall that you can't discern its presence. But then suddenly you do; something clicks in your mind and you immediately realize you can walk into a whole new place that you never thought existed. We call those moments of sudden awareness "epiphanies."

The subject of this discourse is one you're very likely already familiar with; after all, it is the subject of numerous books, songs, masterful pieces of poetry and other forms of creative expression. It is also the subject of innumerable messages from the pulpits of great and small churches all around the globe, and, last but not the least, it is the subject of many controversies. It is at once simple yet intricate, grand but understandable. In spite of its immense popularity, I promise you a few epiphanies. Why am I so sure? I am sure because I write on the subject out of the abundance of my personal, unique experiences with it. It is the subject of the Grace of God.

To experience it personally you will have to make a decision to invite God into your life. When you do that and allow God to place His hand of Grace on your hands, you're in essence inviting Him to take control of your life. To put it more succinctly, you offer your life to God and enter into a profound covenant established unilaterally by God, dating back to a time even before the world was created.

This covenant is unusual compared with natural agreements between two persons because *you have no performance clause* in this arrangement with God. In this covenant God offers you everything: His love, protection, healing for your illnesses, provision for every area of your life and the lives of your loved ones and, most of all, hope. All you have to do is accept God's offer. Of course you have the right to reject it also. It's that simple. The decision is yours to make.

God will not force you to accept His offer. He will not perform summersaults and headstands to lure you—He is God, after all. *You* have to come to Him with both hands stretched out and say, "I surrender myself to You. Take care of me and lead me wherever and however You please."

When you perform this act of submission to the power of the Grace of God, you become qualified to call yourself a prisoner of supernatural abundance, because God's blessings will chase you down at every turn. People will look at you and call you blessed. They will wonder how your children manage to stay out of trouble when all their friends are having babies at the age of fourteen. They will wonder how you keep looking so young when they don't look or feel half as good, and yet they are much younger than you. They may muster up enough courage to ask you how you got the job you have when they've known you twenty years and can't remember you completing college. That's because the Grace of God comes with blessings beyond anything you or I could orchestrate on our own, including a peace that exceeds our human comprehension.

This is not to say that a cloud will swoop down and wait at your side while you mount it, and then take you up into the sky and permanently keep you from the minutiae of the human experience. That's called delusion. I know you don't need me to tell you that. What I'm writing about, though, is real. It's as real as the breaths you're taking right this second, as real as the nose on your face. The Grace of God is powerful and has nothing equal to it that you've ever known. If you've tasted it in your life, then you know what I'm talking about here. If you haven't, then do yourself a humongous favour and ask God for it. It is absolutely free, but you must ask for it. I'll discuss why and how further on. However, before I do that, let me explain a bit about the Grace of God.

Even if you consider yourself a Christian you will want to read this. There are millions of Christians all over the world even today who, in spite of the availability of this knowledge, continue to live their lives without a real understanding of the marvel of the Grace of God. They continue to struggle in every area of their lives, even though some time ago they audibly invited Jesus into their lives to save their souls. When you look closely at their lives in comparison to the lives of ordinary people who either don't know Jesus or don't want to know Him, you find that there are hardly any differences. As a matter of fact, some ordinary people seem to lead better lives! That is not what the Bible says should be happening, because when God created the world according to the Bible, the purpose He established for human beings was to rule and to reign over *everything* that He had created. So if you consider yourself a Christian but don't find yourself living a life that makes people want to ask you questions like "How do you do it?" then you do want to read on.

WHAT IS
THE GRACE OF GOD?

I could get very theological here and give you a thoroughly researched seminary-like description of the subject of the Grace of God, but that will not really help you, unless you are after all a seminary student. I have learned that regardless of the level of your walk with God and in spite of your level of education *and* in spite of your knowledge of theology, the Grace of God is one subject that cannot really be learned.

For instance, I could describe to you the ambrosial and delectable strawberry cheesecake at the Café Mövenpick in downtown Toronto, but you will never have the same "Mama Mia!" moment like I did when I tasted it until you taste it for yourself. You'll have to gently place a morsel of it on your tongue, then gently entrap it between your tongue and the salivated roof of your mouth, then gently move your tongue in a wave-like pattern while it melts, and then resist the temptation to swallow too quickly, so that you don't miss a moment of it. There are no two ways about it.

Fortunately my task is made substantially easy by virtue of the fact that you *have* indeed partaken of the Grace of God on numerous occasions already in your life, even though without necessarily knowing or acknowledging it. Because if it weren't for the operation of the Grace of God in your life at this very instant, you might not be alive even now or have the eyes to see what you are reading or the faculties to understand any of it. Yet here you are. Armed with that knowledge, allow me to articulate to you the meaning of the Grace of God through the experiences of these ordinary individuals.

THE GRACE OF GOD IS HIS FAVOUR

In 1 Samuel we encounter the fascinating story of a shepherd boy who wanted nothing more than to tend to his father's sheep and make music. He would take off alone with the sheep down lonely pastures and deep into the countryside of Bethlehem, where he watched them graze unhurriedly until it was time to take them back home just before dark. He had seven brothers, most of whom were strikingly handsome and very athletic. He seemed like the peculiar one of the bunch and spent long hours just tending his father's flock while either singing to himself or strumming on his harp. He loved the sheep he pastured as though they were members of his family. This young lad had few ambitions besides executing instructions from his father. He had a good heart and cared about people. He was respectful and kind. He was only a teenager, a simple country boy who was happy just to love God and honour his parents. His name was David.

At the time of this narrative in 1 Samuel, Saul was king of Israel. Saul was a haughty and prideful man who disobeyed God repeatedly and offered lame excuses for his actions. He had done it one time too many, and so God turned His face from Saul and withdrew His guardianship of the king. Then God asked the most powerful prophet in Israel to travel to Bethlehem to anoint a new king for Israel. The prophet's name was Samuel, a man so powerful that the Bible says the people of Israel trembled in his presence. The people did not tremble because Samuel was a mighty warrior or a cruel man, but because they knew the anointing of God was upon him. Samuel was God's mouthpiece in Israel in that day. When he spoke the people knew to take him seriously.

Therefore when Samuel walked into Bethlehem that fateful day with a young calf in stride and staff in hand and marched straight to the house of Jesse, the father of Eliab, Abinadab, Shammah and five other boys, the town stood still with expectancy. The people knew something important was about to happen, but no one could imagine what it was.

"Have you come in peace?" the elders of Bethlehem asked him, trembling.

"I have come to offer a sacrifice to the Lord," he responded. Then he added, "Go and purify yourselves and then come join me for the sacrifice."

They scurried off obediently, not daring to ask the prophet any more questions. Samuel ordered Jesse to have all his boys purify themselves as well and to join him for the sacrifice. God had ordered Samuel to the house of Jesse because the one God had appointed to be anointed the new king of Israel was from that humble household.

After the sacrifice Samuel asked Jesse to bring his sons before him one at a time. The deal was that God would speak to Samuel concerning whom to anoint, for even the powerful prophet did not know which one of Jesse's sons God had decided to bestow His favour on. The Bible says that even Samuel was confused. He saw the athletic-looking older sons who had great body posture and striking good looks and thought, "Surely this is the one, Lord." But each time God said, "No," because God knew the thoughts in Samuel's mind. God admonished the prophet, *"Do not look at his appearance or at his physical stature, because I have refused him. For the LORD does not see as man sees; for man looks at the outward appearance, but the LORD looks at the heart"* (1 Samuel 16:7, NKJV).

So it was that after hearing "No" from God seven times, Samuel asked Jesse if those were all his sons. Jesse, himself confused by now, answered that there was one left, but he was only a boy and he was out in the pastures tending to the family's flock. Samuel asked for the boy to be brought before him. As a matter of fact, the prophet indicated that they would remain standing until the boy arrived.

The Bible says that the young David had rosiness in his complexion, perhaps from all the wonderful pure air in the countryside that he enjoyed day after day. He was bright-eyed and very handsome. As soon as he stepped into the house, God spoke to Samuel: "Anoint him." The prophet obeyed.

From that day onward, the power of God was upon the young man. God stayed with him and guided him, directing his path and protecting him from his enemies. David went through many trials and pitfalls throughout his life and made some of the worst mistakes recorded in the Bible. Each time God forgave David. Sometimes God would punish him so that David would straighten up, but God never left his side. The little shepherd boy who loved nothing more than to tend to his father's sheep, strum on his harp, and sing songs of praise to God as he walked the countryside grew to become the greatest king Israel ever had. He had found favour in God's eyes because God looked at his heart and liked what He saw.

POINTS TO REFLECT ON

David loved God and worshipped Him constantly.
David respected his parents and was obedient to them.
David was a hard worker.
David loved and respected other people, even his brothers, who at times treated him unjustly.

THE GRACE OF GOD IS HIS MERCY

In the book of Genesis we encounter the story of an old man. There are accounts of other old men in the book of Genesis, but this old man was special. Unlike the case of the rosy-faced shepherd boy named David, this old man was never described as handsome, talented or athletic. What we do know that distinguishes this man from the people of his time is that the Bible tells us he was "*a just man, perfect in his generations*" (Genesis 6:9). That's a truckload by any standard. He lived long before David's time and lived many more years on the earth than David did. His name was Noah.

In spite of his perfection in the eyes of God, Noah was still an ordinary man who had a wife and children and had to deal with trials and temptations just like you and I face today. Yet he stood unwaveringly on the principles of God, and this caused God to take notice. He refused to allow the news media of his day to cause his beliefs to vacillate like a leaf caught in the wind, landing here one second and who knows where next. Noah did not allow the stresses and the pressures of being a father, husband and provider for his household to cause him to cheat, lie to or slander other people. God looked at him and was pleased. Read how the Bible describes the situation that existed during Noah's day and discern in your imagination what could have been going on:

> *Then the LORD saw that the wickedness of man was great in the earth, and that every intent of the thoughts of his heart was only evil continually. And the LORD was sorry that He had made man on the earth, and He was grieved in His heart. So the LORD said, "I will destroy man whom I have created from the face of the earth, both man and beast, creeping thing and birds of the air, for I am sorry that I have made them." But Noah found grace in the eyes of the LORD.* (Genesis 6:5-8, NKJV)

The God of creation looked at the people He had created and regretted creating them. So He decided to destroy them all, and everything else that breathed, except Noah and his immediate family. You may be scratching your head right now, asking a question similar to the one I asked when I first came across this Bible passage. My question was something like this: "I thought God knew everything from the end and backwards to the beginning. Didn't He know that the people He had created would turn out to be so bad?"

Well, I'm so glad you asked, because the answer is "Yes, He did!" God knew long before He created the world that the people He created would be corrupted by evil. I'll return to the demonstration of God's Grace in and through Noah's life in just a moment, but I'll first give you a bit of Bible study to serve as a backdrop for God's awesome and supernatural ingenuity, ability and capacity. Please allow yourself to be fascinated!

BIBLE STUDY

LESSON 1

The Bible gives us many names that each describes a certain attribute of God. Some of the many names of God include *Yahweh* (meaning "The Lord"—God's personal appellation of Himself), *Jehovah El Shaddai* (meaning "God Almighty"), *Jehovah Rapha* ("God our Healer") and *Jehovah Adonai* ("God our Master"). These names represent unique godly attributes not found in anyone else to the same degree or with the same completeness as God has. To give you some understanding regarding why God has these names, let's look at a simple example.

My wife is *beautiful* to me when we make love. She is *funny* to me when I need cheering up. She is *friendly* when I want to confide in someone. These words actually describe various attributes of my wife's, and I can tap into any one of them when I need to. They are a part of her person and personality, without which she is just another woman in my eyes. Note that the reason these traits are important pertaining to my wife's personality is because they are *personal to me.* Someone else may not think she's that funny. As well, to that person she isn't *friendly* because they don't know her. At the risk of getting myself into serious trouble, I dare say that there is probably one very strange person out there who may not even find her to be beautiful. Why? The answer is that they have no *relationship* with her. The above attributes of my wife's are relevant in terms of how she and I *relate* to each other. That's how they derive their importance. Keep in mind that the fact someone else may not *know* these attributes as they pertain to Naomi doesn't change the fact that they *are.*

Hence the attribute of God described by His name would be the one that you would *relate* to at the time of your particular need. That is the name that would be *important* to you at that particular time. This does not minimize His other attributes, but rather magnifies the one you need.

For instance, in Genesis 22:13-14, when Abraham needed a ram to offer to God as a sacrifice *in place of* Isaac, his beloved son, on Mount Moriah and God came through and provided the ram, Abraham named the place *Jehovah Jireh.* That name is dedicated to God's supreme and unique ability and capacity to supernaturally provide all our needs at precisely the right moment. The name *Jehovah Rapha* would not have been much good to Abraham at the time because Abraham needed *provision* and not healing.

In Revelation 22:13, God called Himself *"the Alpha and the Omega."* This is the name of God that describes His omniscience, which is the fact that He knows everything from the beginning to the end. This *Alpha and Omega* is the God I'll be discussing with you.

He knew from the very beginning of time and long before He decided to create the world that His crown jewel—that being humankind—would turn its back on Him one day. He knew that humankind would deny Him, distrust Him, lie to Him and even start worshipping idols. God knew that the day would come when He would have to destroy all that He had created in order to purify the generations that would follow. He knew this because He created us. The question then is this: Why did He go ahead with such a heartbreaking endeavour? Why would one wish to endure such disappointment and pain?

Where God is concerned, the answer is *love.* God loves us with an unending love. He loves us with the same purity, expectancy and excitement that parents lavish on even their unborn children. We lavish them with this deep love even though experience tells us that the day will come when they will lie to us, insult us, abandon us, steal from us and even disown us sometimes. In spite of this fore-knowledge, we, like God, go ahead and have children anyway! Again, the reason is because we love them.

Since I believe that you are a thinker, the next question you may be asking may sound like this: "If God knew the ultimate outcome of humankind's frail loyalties, why didn't He create us so that we would be incapable of such evil?"

Once again, where God is concerned the answer is *love.* If you're scratching your head in bewilderment it means you're on the right track. If you're nodding your head in agreement then you too are on the right track. The answer lies in God's description of love and not the horrifically poor replica human beings have created in their sinful and imperfect state.

Let's take a look then at God's kind of love as communicated in His Word, the Bible. Read this incredible passage from I Corinthians 13 written by the great apostle Paul by divine inspiration. This is the man who wrote about a third of the New Testament:

> *If I speak in the tongues of men and of angels, but have not love, I am only a resounding gong or a clanging cymbal. If I have the gift of prophecy and can fathom all mysteries and all knowledge, and if I have a faith that can move mountains, but have not love, I am nothing. If I give all I possess to the poor and surrender my body to the flames, but have not love, I gain nothing. Love is patient, love is kind. It does not envy, it does not boast, it is not*

proud. It is not rude, it is not self-seeking, it is not easily angered, it keeps no record of wrongs. Love does not delight in evil but rejoices with the truth. It always protects, always trusts, always hopes, {and} always perseveres. (I Corinthians 13:1-7, NIV)

As you can immediately tell, this is not the kind of love perpetuated by the motion picture industry, most of the book publishing industry and certainly not from the music industry right around the world. The standard for love established and adhered to by God is humanly unachievable. At best you strive to emulate God's love, because that is what you and I ought to do.

Therefore as a parent and as a child of God,

You *ought* to be patient with your children and the people around you.
You *ought* to control your anger and not burst into uncontrollable tirades.
You *ought* not to be boastful.
You *ought* to forgive those who cause you pain.
You *ought* to protect the ones you love.
You *ought* to trust that all will be well and have hope that it will be so.

You will never be able to do it as well as God does, but I bet you know deep down in your heart that this is the way it *should* be. The test to confirm in your mind that this *is* the way it should be is to ask yourself *how* you would like others to relate to you in the areas mentioned.

The language of *ought* is the language of aspiration. This is the language that propels a human being towards that which is good. Hence, even though most of us aren't quite there yet in terms of our moral and ethical configuration, there is no denying that it is definitely the direction to be heading in.

Remember the question we asked that instigated this discourse: "If God knew the ultimate outcome of humankind's frail loyalties, why didn't He create us so that we would be incapable of such evil?"

The answer, like I mentioned, is because of love. That is, *God's kind of love*. It is the kind of love you give even when it hurts. It is the kind of love you give because you know it is the right thing to do. It is the kind of love you give because you simply ought to. When you act because you *ought* to, you are exercising your fundamental God-given right of choice, because you can *choose* to do what you *ought* to do in order to please God, or not.

Inherent in the human ability to make choices is the ability to choose to act because it is simply the right thing to do even though it may not be the most convenient. When you do some things because you *ought* to therefore, like deciding to know God for example, or deciding to know Him in a deeper way, you approach life at a level uncommon to the masses. To use another example, when you give to the needy because it is simply the right thing to do and not just because you have spare change and want to feel good about yourself, you too approach life from an uncommon angle; you approach life a little like God. I propose to you that *there can be no love in the absence of the prerogative of choice*. In the same way that you wouldn't want to be married to someone if that individual feels coerced into marrying you, God does not want to be in relationship with anyone who doesn't have the ability to reject Him. When a person has the ability to reject you but instead makes the choice to be with you, you can say that that person loves you. That is the kind of love God has for us and wants in return. He loves us so much that He had to give us the ability to reject Him. Otherwise we would be robots. Robots can't think independently or beyond the model of *cause and effect*. They can't sympathize, rejoice, endure with or love you. I don't want to be married to a robot, so I know that God wouldn't want to be related to one.

Even though God knew ahead of time that we would one day

reject Him and fall short of His divine standard, He went ahead to love and create us anyway.

LESSON 2

Genesis is one of the five books of the Old Testament written by Moses thousands of years before the coming of Jesus. The other four are the books of Exodus, Leviticus, Numbers and Deuteronomy. Combined they are called the *Torah* and comprise the foundation of the Jewish faith. Moses wrote Genesis by the revelation and inspiration of God, about an era even before his time. In the other books such as Exodus, there are accounts he wrote that were derived from the Hebrew experience as a whole, learned from the generations before him. And as you will notice when you read the Torah in its entirety, Moses himself was one of the major characters. He had firsthand knowledge concerning what he wrote about. He wrote as a living witness in those instances.

Moses had a good life, having been raised in the house of the ruler of Egypt, the pharaoh who ruled most of the known world in his day. With such privileged upbringing came a good education. But by all accounts Moses was not a sophisticated academician. As a matter of fact, there is biblical evidence indicating a shortness of confidence in his own abilities, which could have emanated from a lack of accomplishment in his personal life before his supernatural encounter with God. In spite of those personal shortcomings, Moses was called by God for very high service in His kingdom, and Moses delivered God's people from four hundred years of bondage in Egypt. This narrative is played out in Exodus.

Notwithstanding the obvious lack of academic prowess demon-strated in Moses' life, some of the books of the Old Testament that he wrote have embedded in them an amazing depth of syntactic coding so sophisticated that even modern-day computers would be hard pressed to replicate it. However, as impressive as the syntactic codes found in Genesis are, for instance, they are only a part of an even more elaborate network of Bible codes that theologians and Bible scholars such as Dr. Chuck Missler (author of *Learning the Bible in 24 Hours*) and others have come to call *Bible authentication codes.* These codes leave even the hardest of doubters wondering "what if?"

Here is what I mean: when Moses wrote the five books of the Torah, he knew God was directing him. However, he did not know that over three thousand years later people in our generation would discover these powerful syntactic codes that he was in no way qualified to have conceived and embedded into the texts he had written. While Moses wrote, like many other writers of the Bible, God Himself embedded and integrated sophisticated layers of syntactic codes to serve as evidence of *purpose and design,* to authenticate the final authority of His Word, so that this doubtful and sinful generation of human beings could anchor to it and direct themselves to Him.

A powerful instance of evidence of this integrated design is found in Genesis 5, where Adam's genealogy is described:

This is the written account of Adam's line. When God created man, he made him in the likeness of God. He created them male and female and blessed them. And when they were created, he called them "man."

*When Adam had lived 130 years, he had a son in his own likeness, in his own image; and he named him **Seth**. After Seth was born, Adam lived 800 years and had other sons and daughters. Altogether, Adam lived 930 years, and then he died.*

*When Seth had lived 105 years, he became the father of **Enosh**. And after he became the father of Enosh, Seth lived 807 years and had other sons and daughters. Altogether, Seth lived 912 years, and then he died.*

When Enosh had lived 90 years, he became the father of **Kenan**. And after he became the father of Kenan, Enosh lived 815 years and had other sons and daughters. Altogether, Enosh lived 905 years, and then he died.

When Kenan had lived 70 years, he became the father of **Mahalalel**. And after he became the father of Mahalalel, Kenan lived 840 years and had other sons and daughters. Altogether, Kenan lived 910 years, and then he died.

When Mahalalel had lived 65 years, he became the father of **Jared**. And after he became the father of Jared, Mahalalel lived 830 years and had other sons and daughters. Altogether, Mahalalel lived 895 years, and then he died.

When Jared had lived 162 years, he became the father of **Enoch**. And after he became the father of Enoch, Jared lived 800 years and had other sons and daughters. Altogether, Jared lived 962 years, and then he died.

When Enoch had lived 65 years, he became the father of **Methuselah**. And after he became the father of Methuselah, Enoch walked with God 300 years and had other sons and daughters. Altogether, Enoch lived 365 years. Enoch walked with God; then he was no more, because God took him away.

When Methuselah had lived 187 years, he became the father of **Lamech**. And after he became the father of Lamech, Methuselah lived 782 years and had other sons and daughters. Altogether, Methuselah lived 969 years, and then he died.

When Lamech had lived 182 years, he had a son. He named him **Noah** and said, "He will comfort us in the labor and painful toil of our hands caused by the ground the LORD has cursed." After Noah was born, Lamech lived 595 years and had other sons and daughters. Altogether, Lamech lived 777 years, and then he died.

After Noah was 500 years old, he became the father of Shem, Ham and Japheth. (NIV, emphasis added)

THE EVIDENCE

This is the evidence God left in this chapter of His incredible omniscience.

First of all, the listing of the names of Adam and his genealogy up to Noah tells a story. In the Hebrew language *Adam* means "man," *Seth* means "appointed," *Enosh* means "mortal," *Kenan* means "sorrow," *Mahalalel* means "the Blessed God," *Jared* means "shall come down" *Enoch* means "teaching," *Methuselah* means "His death shall bring," *Lamech* means "the despairing" and *Noah* means "comfort." When you piece this all together, what is derived sounds like this: "Man [is] appointed mortal sorrow [but] the Blessed God shall come down teaching. His death shall bring the despairing comfort."

Absolutely mind-blowing!

Secondly and very importantly the story is prophetic. It foretold of God's redemptive plan for humankind and how He would send His one and only son to the cross to die so that we would be reconciled to Him. That was exactly what happened when Jesus came down from heaven and allowed Himself to be killed and hung on a cross to die. He made that unimaginable sacrifice to bring us comfort in the reunion with God, our Father and Maker. It is by far the greatest search-and-rescue mission of all time.

One of the most powerful aspects of the Bible is its ability to tell the future before it happens. For instance, Daniel foretold the reunification of the Jewish people 2500 years before it happened! That's the kind of information that shuts the mouths of critics. No other book in the world has demonstrated this ability.

So now then, back to the demonstration of God's mercy by His Grace in and through the life of an "insane" old man. That's how the people of Noah's day described him because he dared to be different and to trust God against all odds. God chose this simple man named Noah to be the connecting link that would perpetuate His creation at a time when destruction of every living creature was God's major preoccupation. God knew He would use Noah even *before* He began creating the world. Talk of a demonstration of mercy! And in *God-style* God did not end there. He orchestrated things so that this same man's name would conclude the greatest prophecy of all, which foretold of the descending of God to earth in human form to execute the most illustrious search-and-rescue operation the world will ever know. You have to agree with me that when God honours you, He does a really good job of it.

You are alive and well today in spite of all that you have been through! Yes indeed, God is a merciful God.

THE GRACE OF GOD IS HIS PROVISION

God created the world and everything that is in it, from the ground we walk on to the sky above our heads and everything in between. This is how David put it in Psalm 19:1-4:

The heavens declare the glory of God;
the skies proclaim the work of his hands.
Day after day they pour forth speech;
night after night they display knowledge.
There is no speech or language
where their voice is not heard.
Their voice goes out into all the earth,
their words to the ends of the world. (NIV)

What David is saying is that everywhere you turn there is evidence of the magnificence of God's handiwork, and if you look closely enough you will even see His imprint on them, carved into their DNA. In every language and in every tongue, from one end of the earth to the other, there is plenty of visual support for the presence of deliberateness and design that point to God's handiwork.

From the very beginning He made human beings to rule and to reign over everything He had created. We were to harvest food from the land, from the sea and from the air. God gave Adam and Eve everything they needed to live well in the Garden of Eden. Even though they blew it by disobeying God and inviting His punishment, God did not stop providing for them. God even continued to provide for the Hebrew people, the descendants of Abraham, thousands of years later after they thoughtlessly turned their backs on Him right after He rescued them from servitude and bondage in Egypt, which they were in for four hundred years.

Even today God continues to provide for His creation.

Something that I thank God for is the fact that even those who still refuse to allow Him into their lives are beneficiaries of this provision. If it weren't for that Grace, many of us wouldn't be alive long enough to get to know God. When the seasons come and go and cause the crops of the fields to grow for food, both those who believe in God and those who shun Him reap the benefits. When night falls so that our bodies should rest in order to be refreshed, all of God's creation partakes of that gift. That is His Grace, but many still take it for granted.

The secular world would like us to believe that there was a "big bang" several billion years ago that resulted in the universe we know and ultimately you and me. Apparently we were once tadpoles and baboons and over time evolved to the fine species we now are. Along the way we learned to build skyscrapers, make airplanes and decipher the intricate network of human physiology. Buying into such falsehood requires that you agree that there was no comprehensive design from the beginning of the world and that the fact that nature perfectly supports our existence by providing us with food and oxygen is just coincidence. Of course anyone who believes that must also believe that you can win the New York State lottery every day for two years. Or that there's a chance that a grade 2 pupil can perform successful heart surgery. Or perhaps that you can successfully walk a tightrope across the Niagara Falls gorge with your eyes closed. That obviously doesn't make any sense.

However, this should make some sense to you: God is a scientist and indeed orchestrated the entire universe purposefully and with engineering precision so that we can rest knowing that things will work predictably. The sun rises in the morning and sets in the evening day in and day out. The moon works the nightshift with unquestionable loyalty and has done so since the first night was *spoken* into being by God. The seasons come and go, bringing with them harvests, beauty, expectancy and hope. There is no randomness in what we experience, especially when we don't interfere with God's handiwork. This is the stuff of mechanics, the hallmark of science. It is the manifestation of God's omniscience, which is beyond anything humankind can replicate.

God worked out every possible mathematical and scientific equation and formula needed to make the world work like a well-oiled machine. From the simple leaf that is blown seemingly without purpose off the tree branch to the various seasons of the year and the seamless functioning of the intricate network of planets, stars and galaxies that hang without visible support high up in the sky, they are all part of an overwhelmingly complex scheme completely knowable only to the one who made them.

That explains why we continue to "discover" new parts of the cosmos on a fairly regular basis even to this day, hundreds of years since humankind started methodically studying the cosmos. We can only learn of God's overall scheme in small parts at a time, to coincide with His agenda for humanity and its destiny. Human discoveries and inventions are nothing more than the Maker revealing bits and pieces of Himself to us, until the day the complete extent of His Glory will be made known to us. Revelation offers an intriguing and fearfully wonderful read on the subject of the revealing of the fullness of God's Glory. I encourage you to study it carefully if you haven't done so yet.

God has given each one of us a very small piece of a very large puzzle. Each properly laid down piece gives us a better glimpse of His magnificence and of His Grace. We place our pieces where He wants them without being able to grasp hold of the complete picture, because it is much too large for us to comprehend.

Imagine an army of ants each delivering a blade of grass to the centre of a football field. The area is so large to the tiny ants that it is impossible for them to perceive the entire topography of the field. Yet as each one of them places its tiny blade of grass, over time they will slowly but surely fill up the entire area of the football field. Conceivably they may never know just how much they've accomplished, because they will be unable to perceive the full picture from their terrestrial position.

But one day, as the Bible declares, Jesus will return to take His people up to heaven with Him. This is what the apostle Paul says in I Thessalonians: *"After that, we who are still alive and are left will be caught up together with them in the clouds to meet the Lord in the air. And so we will be with the Lord forever"* (4:17, NIV).

Imagine the amazement when the little ants are lifted up three hundred feet so that they can now perceive the completed wonder of their seemingly meaningless endeavours. The story that follows will add some dimension to the point I'm making.

The great grandmother of King David (of whom I wrote earlier on in the chapter) was a Moabite widow named Ruth. She was so insignificant in the early days of her life that there is no account of that part of her biography anywhere in the Bible. Even as she gave birth to King David's grandfather, a man named Obed, she had no idea that she had been handpicked by God to perpetuate the lineage that the Messiah of the world would come from. She had absolutely no idea that her blade of grass in the middle of the football field would be the one that the *Bread of Life* would grow from.

The Bible tells us in Ruth that in the days when sin and strife abounded in Israel, a famine crept into the land and forced a man named Elimelech to sell his property and move with his family to a neighbouring country named Moab so that they wouldn't perish from starvation. Life in Moab was fine until Elimelech died and left his wife, Naomi, a widow. Elimelech and Naomi had two sons, Mahlon and Chilion, who also eventually died in Moab, leaving behind their widows. The widows were named Orpah and Ruth. Their mother-in-law, Naomi, grieved terribly for her incredible misfortune.

Life in Moab was becoming just as hard as it had been in Israel during the famine. One day news came to Naomi that back at home the land was fertile once again and there was peace and provision. So even though she really had nothing to return to Israel for, such as immediate family members or possessions, she decided that it would be better to die in her homeland instead of in a foreign country like her husband and sons had.

Once she made up her mind, Naomi informed her two daughters-in-law and packed up what little belongings she had. To her surprise both Orpah and Ruth insisted on abandoning their homeland and their families and following Naomi to Israel, even though they knew she was returning to certain destitution.

Their decision met with castigation from Naomi, who was a loving, selfless woman. She loved both her daughters-in-law to the point that she had to sternly insist that they start new lives in their homeland and let her return to her own homeland to face whatever fate awaited her. After much crying and admonishing, Naomi finally convinced Orpah to stay. Ruth, on the other hand, was relentless. This is what she said to her mother-in-law:

> *Entreat me not to leave you,*
> *Or to turn back from following after you;*
> *For wherever you go, I will go;*
> *And wherever you lodge, I will lodge;*
> *Your people shall be my people,*

And your God, my God.
Where you die, I will die,
And there will I be buried.
The LORD do so to me, and more also,
If anything but death parts you and me. (Ruth 1:16-17,
NKJV)

Naomi became speechless after she discerned that Ruth's resolve was unshakable. So both women returned to Israel, where they toiled, some days going without any food to eat, until one day Ruth went into the countryside, on the prompting of Naomi, to pick up after the harvesters of the grain fields so that whatever they dropped Ruth could bring home for dinner. Ruth happened to wander into the grain field of a man named Boaz, who was a rich relative of Naomi's. Boaz took a liking to Ruth, and they eventually married, giving birth to Obed, who became the father of Jesse, who was the father of the shepherd boy who became the greatest king Israel ever had. From the lineage of King David would be born the Messiah of the world, the Lord Jesus Christ.

God's amazing Grace orchestrated provision for an ordinary woman, Ruth, and pulled her from the clutches of destitution and starvation to the blessings of His abundance. Once again in *God-style* God did not end there, but crowned Ruth with the singular privilege of being the great grandmother of Jesus Christ, the one around whom all of history revolve.

THE GRACE OF GOD IS UNMERITED

In the opening pages of this book I mentioned a unique and paradoxical covenant that you enter into with God when you sincerely invite Him into your life to be Lord and Master and to take control of all the things that concern you. A normal covenant is an agreement and it is usually between two or more persons, each of whom would have rights and obligations based on the agreement.

The paradox in this agreement with God is in the fact that you are the beneficiary but you have absolutely no performance obligations under the covenant. Therefore, even though it is an agreement between two parties, God *unilaterally* dictates the terms, makes you the beneficiary and absolves you of all obligations! All that is expected of you is that you accept it. But when you accept this offer God puts before you by His Grace, you cease to live for yourself. You cease to be your own person and you give up your "rights" to everything in the world, including your life. In a sense you become a prisoner of God's Grace. You become a captive of His unending love. Your life becomes God's property.

I know that sounds a bit hard to swallow for many people. In fact many years ago I would laugh out loud and knock my glass down from the table in the process at the very concept of surrendering my life to God. But one fine day He put His searchlights out on me, like He does for millions of people around the world, and when I allowed Him to He arrested my soul into salvation for my own good. My life has never been the same since, and I thank Him with all my heart.

Abraham, our *Father of Faith*, entered into one such paradoxical and unilateral agreement with God, which required him to do nothing but walk on the red carpet of Grace that God rolled out before him and to enter into the benefits of the provisos of the covenant. This is the account of that powerful event documented in Genesis:

> After these things the word of the LORD came to Abram in a vision, saying, "Do not be afraid, Abram. I am your shield, your exceedingly great reward."
>
> But Abram said, "Lord GOD, what will You give me, seeing I go childless, and the heir of my house is Eliezer of Damascus?" Then Abram said, "Look, You have given me no offspring; indeed one born in my house is my heir!"

And behold, the word of the LORD came to him, saying, "This one shall not be your heir, but one who will come from your own body shall be your heir." Then He brought him outside and said, "Look now toward heaven, and count the stars if you are able to number them." And He said to him, "So shall your descendants be."

And he believed in the LORD, and He accounted it to him for righteousness. Then He said to him, "I am the LORD, who brought you out of Ur of the Chaldeans, to give you this land to inherit it."

And he said, "Lord GOD, how shall I know that I will inherit it?"

So He said to him, "Bring Me a three-year-old heifer, a three-year-old female goat, a three-year-old ram, a turtledove, and a young pigeon." Then he brought all these to Him and cut them in two, down the middle, and placed each piece opposite the other; but he did not cut the birds in two. And when the vultures came down on the carcasses, Abram drove them away. **Now when the sun was going down, a deep sleep fell upon Abram;** and behold, horror and great darkness fell upon him. Then He said to Abram: "Know certainly that your descendants will be strangers in a land that is not theirs, and will serve them, and they will afflict them four hundred years. And also the nation whom they serve I will judge; afterward they shall come out with great possessions. Now as for you, you shall go to your fathers in peace; you shall be buried at a good old age. But in the fourth generation they shall return here, for the iniquity of the Amorites is not yet complete."

And it came to pass, when the sun went down and it was dark, that behold, there appeared a smoking oven and a burning torch that passed between those pieces. On the same day the LORD made a covenant with Abram, saying:

To your descendants I have given this land, from the river of

Egypt to the great river, the River Euphrates—the Kenites, the Kenezzites, the Kadmonites, the Hittites, the Perizzites, the Rephaim, the Amorites, the Canaanites, the Girgashites, and the Jebusites. (Genesis 15:1-21, NKJV, emphasis added)

God asked Abraham to make the necessary preparations for a traditional Hebrew covenant that two parties would enter into, but then He put Abraham to sleep and performed the covenant rituals by Himself. When Abraham woke up, all that was left to do was for him to either reject God's offer or, like he wisely did, accept it. The entire history and future of the Jewish people has been and will continue to be guided by that unique agreement God entered into with Abraham on that day.

If you're an inquisitive person—and I pray that you are—then you're probably already asking this question: "From the sound of it, God predestined the shepherd boy David, the old man Noah, the young destitute widow named Ruth and our Father of Faith, Abraham, to benefit from His Grace. What then are the criteria for qualifying for such an incredible privilege?"

The short answer is this: Nobody qualifies. There are no criteria for selection. There is nothing anyone could do to qualify for the Grace of God, because God's standard of purity and obedience is absolute, and no human being can live up to it in their own strength. You know that if you're a human being, then you sin. That's the nature you and I were born with, which we each inherited from Adam, since he took sides with Lucifer in the Garden of Eden and distrusted God in the process. It was only for a short time, but it was enough to contaminate his posterity for the rest of time. That is the source of our sin nature and the reason why there is nothing you or I can do to qualify for God's Grace. It makes no difference how much you love God or for how long you've served Him. If you lie about anything or break fellowship with God or lust after anything that puts a fence between you and God, then

SAM TITA

you know you cannot qualify. There isn't a human being alive who doesn't sin at least once in a while.

David was handpicked by God, but he committed some of the most atrocious acts recorded in the entire Bible, from murder to adultery.

Abraham, our great Father of Faith, laughed at God when He promised to give him a son in his old age. Abraham did not believe God! What a great irony, considering that he ultimately became such a deep believer in God that he was prepared to offer that son back to God as a sacrifice.

Ruth, the great grandmother of King David, came from an idolatrous and cultic background and was herself a practitioner for a long time. The list could become very long if I attempted to enumerate the instances when many of God's chosen people fell very short of His standards.

If you feel like throwing your hands up in the air and shouting "I give up!" then you're nearly at the point where you need to be. This is what I mean: you need to get to a point where you can't figure it out on your own and so you give up trying and instead ask God to reveal His Grace to you personally. If you sincerely want to know, God will reveal Himself to you.

In II Kings some enemies of Israel besieged the prophet Elisha at dawn while he and his servant still slept, because by revelation from God he thwarted their plans to invade Israel on several occasions. When he woke up in the morning and realized their predicament, Elisha's servant was terrified by what he saw and asked the prophet what to do. With deliberate ease Elisha asked him not to worry, because their enemies were outnumbered. Of course the servant thought his master had lost his mind, because when he looked around all he saw was the battle-ready battalion of the Syrian army waiting to capture the prophet. So Elisha asked God to open his servant's eyes so that he would see why he (the prophet) was so calm under the circumstances. God responded. This is how the passage describes it: *"And Elisha prayed, and said, ' LORD, I pray, open his eyes that he may see.' Then the LORD opened the eyes of the young man, and he saw. And behold, the mountain was full of horses and chariots of fire all around Elisha"* (II Kings 6:17, NKJV).

Whether by revelation or by frustration, you have to get to the point of surrender, because surrendering to God is the only prerequisite to deliberately enter into His Grace. There is no other way. God has done everything needed for you and me to partake of His Grace, but you have to want it, then you have to ask for it, and finally you have to accept it when He offers it to you.

There are millions of Christians today who have known God for many years but still don't understand the miracle of His Grace. They read their Bibles, attend church regularly and even serve God in various capacities. Yet they haven't surrendered to Him! They manipulate the people in their lives in order to achieve what they want instead of praying for God's intervention. Sometimes they have really good intentions but go about achieving their results the wrong way. For instance, a woman should not pray for her husband to get into relationship with God and then deny him sex until he starts reading his Bible or attending church. That is most ungodly. In fact, the Bible calls that witchcraft! That's how bad that is. On the other hand, a husband should not stop supporting his unemployed wife because he thinks she isn't looking for work as diligently as she should. He should instead do everything to enable her search and then pray harder than he ever did so that she will find work.

Surrendering to God means that you do all you can in love and then wait on God to cause it to manifest in His time. To enable you to completely hand your issues over to God, He makes this promise in the book of Isaiah: *"But those who wait on the LORD Shall renew their strength; They shall mount up with wings like eagles, They shall run and not be weary, They shall walk and not faint"* (Isaiah 40:31, NKJV).

I have said this before, but I'll say it again: God has done it all for us. All that is left is for you to accept it. He knows that sometimes we get impatient and want to take matters into our own hands, so He gave us this Scripture passage and others like it to hold on to so that we know that He knows what we're going through.

In my own life, in the summer of 2006, I returned to Canada from the United States to begin rebuilding my broken family. I'd lived and travelled in various parts of the United States for nearly two of the five years during which Naomi and I had been separated. I was full of elation and expectancy that summer.

I still had some pending personal issues that I was yet to wrap up in the United States, but I was thankful that God had answered my prayers to reunite me with my family. In God-style He didn't just stop there either; He put a fresh love in my heart for Naomi, from whom I had been separated for over five years. I'd also declared publicly that not even death would reunite Naomi and I because of the many issues that at the time I believed were wrong with her. Therefore when God placed this new love in my heart for this dear woman it was as though I'd fallen in love with her for the very first time. With premonition I asked her if she would want me back, and lo and behold she said "Yes"!

Nothing could be better. But by the time I got back to Canada she had fallen madly in love with someone she had been attending school with and had known for a short time. She was just recovering from 30 years of being pillaged by anxiety, and the stress of her college program literally drove her into the arms of this guy. I couldn't believe my eyes. I knew that she loved me because she expressed that to me, but I'd arrived just a little late to offer her the emotional support she desperately needed at the time.

There I was, ready and excited about all that the future held for me and my family. Yet the woman with whom that sparkling new future was going to be with was in love with someone else. I was tempted to return to previous relationships, because I was very good at that sort of thing. I was tempted to confront the man

Naomi was seeing. I was very tempted to seek out an affair to console myself until Naomi came to her senses. I was drawn like a magnet to online pornography, from which I'd been delivered only about a year before. I cried out to God as I considered each of those temptations. I'd already done them all before and knew that I didn't want to go down any of those roads again. I spent many nights at home alone because Naomi, whom God had asked me to return to and who had declared to me that she still loved me and to whom I had returned with a fresh and powerful new love, had to spend the night at her friend's place.

I was hurting beyond anything I'd ever experienced up to then, but I didn't tell anyone. Naomi knew what I was going through and wanted to make things right, but somehow she seemed powerless in the emotion she had for this fellow. I couldn't talk to anyone about it because I didn't want to put my wife in the spotlight for the wrong reasons. Isaiah 40:31 was one of the Scriptures I grabbed on to. I would praise and worship God deep into the night in those painful times. I cried out to Him, many nights curled up on the floor, until I fell asleep. I determined not to do anything that would offend God but to wait on Him.

I knew I needed help to keep from falling into one or several of those temptations that lurked at the gates of my mind. Therefore I asked God for help. Above all the things that I cried to Him for during that time was the Grace to wait on Him.

Then one night several months later it happened. Naomi and I were having a conversation when her friend's name came up. She said, "I find him so annoying."

If you know Naomi, then you know she is a gentle spirit. She does not easily utter that combination of words about anyone unless it is serious. Naturally my ears pricked right up as the impact of those five words settled in. We spoke for several hours that night, and that chapter closed permanently in both our lives. For a guy who had abandoned his wife and children and broken many hearts along the way, God's amazing Grace had zeroed in on my life, even though you might agree that I really didn't deserve it. That very same package I got from God for free is available to you today if you want to take advantage of the offer, and I pray that you do.

DIGGING DEEPER

2

This exposition is by no means an exhaustive study of the subject of the Grace of God. It is really not intended to be, as a matter of fact. The plan is to get you to a point where you understand just enough to take advantage of it. I've been around training and development a long time, and one of the more ubiquitous mistakes I've encountered is where people acquire so much information that they become heavy with it and ultimately fail to use it.

Many Christians have become academicians and theologians instead of doers and witnesses for Jesus. This book is intended to compel you to do something with what you learn, and not merely to educate you. To that extent therefore I want you to consider the following trigger questions:

Do you understand the nature of the Grace of God?
Do you understand how to leverage the Grace of God?
Are you presently experiencing the Grace of God in your life?
Can you give an account of that experience?

While you mull over these questions also consider these commonalities present in every manifestation of the Grace of God.

GOD'S LOVE

Underlying every instance of God's Grace is His love. This amazing Grace of God is only possible because His love for us has no limits. How else could He save a guy like me who was a champion in the camp of the devil prior to encountering Him? How else could He have continued walking with David even after David committed murder and adultery? How else could He sit back and watch His precious son get tormented and hung on a cross to die just so that He would be reunited with a creation that had turned its back on Him over and over again? God's love is embedded in His Grace. The two are inseparable.

GOD'S FAITHFULNESS

God's faithfulness is evident in every instance of the manifestation of His Grace. I John 1:9 states, *"If we confess our sins, He is faithful and just to forgive us our sins and to cleanse us from all unrighteousness"* (NKJV).

The following is the foremost definition of the word *faithful* from the Oxford English Dictionary: Remaining loyal and steadfast.

God's faithfulness is loyal and steadfast. What He promises to do He does, and He never fails. God is completely reliable. The Bible tells us that He never changes. He is the same yesterday, today and forever. Therefore we can count on Him and all His promises to us. He will move kings and presidents, change weather patterns and places just to bring about a promise He made to you. This has been true in my life.

Several years ago Naomi and I invested a substantial portion of our personal resources into a business that was going nowhere fast. We made many sacrifices in our lifestyle just to give the business the opportunity to grow. Our idea was a good one, because it was working for other people. We had the human resources and expertise to make it work, but the economic times were harsh and the competition had become very fierce. We generated revenues, but they were just enough to sustain the business. Things had gotten so dire that we missed paying three instalments of the condominium management fees for our town home. The total amount due was only about six hundred dollars. After the third payment was missed the condominium management company hired a lawyer according to the bylaws of the condominium and took us to court. What had started out being just six hundred dollars dollars quickly became thousands. They placed a lien on our home and gave us three weeks to pay up or they would foreclose.

Of course as you read you're probably asking yourself why we didn't just borrow the six hundred dollars dollars in the first place and avoid having to pay so much more afterwards. The short answer is that we had tapped out every resource available to us at the time. We were on our own with only God beside us. So we cried out to Him. We were painfully aware of the fact that we had chosen to get into business and were not coerced. This was our doing and not anyone else's. In spite of the foregoing, we came crying to God because there was nowhere else to go at that point. I faced the real possibility of having to explain to my children and my wife how we ended up on the street when we didn't have to. I had put my family at risk, even though my intentions were very noble and I had a successful background in other areas.

One day in the summer of 2007 I was driving back to the office from a sales appointment. I was on Highway 401, known to be the busiest highway in all of North America, with average daily volumes surpassing 500,000 cars. Traffic was light at the time, so most cars were easily exceeding the posted speed limit of 100 kilometres an hour. But then suddenly and unexpectedly traffic slowed down to a crawl just for about half a minute.

I was bopping my head and praising God to the music of Shekinah Glory Ministries. I turned my head to my right for a moment, and my eyes locked with those of Huey, a former stock-broker colleague from nearly a decade prior. Both our faces lit up, and we started yelling greetings at each other. Huey called out his cell phone number to me, and I entered it into my keypad as traffic opened up and he sped off in his black convertible BMW.

As soon as I got off the highway I called Huey. We chatted for only about five minutes, during which time he invited me to come to his office the next day to discuss a project that he was involved with. I cancelled everything on my calendar and drove down to Huey's office the next day and met with the project manager. I had my resume in hand and was dressed and prepared for an interview.

Bill, the project manager, spent half the time I was there with both his legs on the boardroom table, reclining in a large leather boardroom chair while talking with his girlfriend on his cell phone. He beckoned me to sit down without as much as looking my way. When he finally got off the phone, he shook my hand, brushed aside my resume and asked me when I could start. He said that if Huey recommended me, I had to be good enough.

Five weeks later I'd made $25,000, redeemed our home from the auction block and even paid off some other debts. God came through for me and my family even though I messed up. He rearranged the flow of 500,000 cars on Highway 401 on that day so that I would arrive at that particular spot to meet with Huey. Any single change in any of Huey's or my activities prior to that moment would have prevented that meeting. If one set of traffic lights on the street had come on too early or too late for either Huey or me, that divinely appointed meeting would never have occurred. I believe that God saw the intentions of my heart and might have been pleased with the fact that in spite of the dire nature of our predicament I still praised Him radically and openly.

His faithfulness is indeed thorough, true and steady in spite of our shortcomings. Like I mentioned earlier, He will rearrange the world just to orchestrate things to line up for you, because the Bible says that if we seek God diligently He will surely reward us.

Remember these:

Even when it is your fault, run to God.

Surrender the issue completely to Him.

Pray and ask God for the grace to wait on Him. Don't do anything rash or illegal.

While you wait on Him, praise and thank Him for what He has already done.

GOD'S SOVEREIGNTY

God is sovereign above everything in the world. He is even above the laws of nature, because those laws have their source in Him. He is above everything created, because all of creation has its source in Him. The account of how God created the world is found in the opening chapter of Genesis. God literally spoke the world into being. His words have the ability to form things as He utters them. There is no one else in the world like God. He can speak things and circumstances into your life, and can speak them out as well. He alone can do and undo anything at any time. That is how He is able to disregard the laws of retribution and point the floodlight of His Grace into any area of your life at precisely the moment when you think there is no way out.

For instance, in Isaiah there is the fascinating story of how God reversed the movement of the sun as a sign to a devoted believer that his life had been extended:

In those days Hezekiah was sick and near death. And Isaiah the prophet, the son of Amoz, went to him and said to him, "Thus says the LORD: 'Set your house in order, for you shall die and not live.'"

Then Hezekiah turned his face toward the wall, and prayed to the LORD, and said, "Remember now, O LORD, I pray, how I have walked before You in truth and with a loyal heart, and have done what is good in Your sight." And Hezekiah wept bitterly.

And the word of the LORD came to Isaiah, saying, "Go and tell Hezekiah, 'Thus says the LORD, the God of David your father: "I have heard your prayer, I have seen your tears; surely I will add to your days fifteen years. I will deliver you and this city from the hand of the king of Assyria, and I will defend this city."' And this is the sign to you from the LORD, that the LORD will do this thing which He has spoken: Behold, I will bring the shadow on the sundial, which has gone down with the sun on the sundial of Ahaz, ten degrees backward." So the sun returned ten degrees on the dial by which it had gone down. (38:1-8, NKJV)

In all the accounts of the manifestation of God's Grace that I described, and as you will find when you reflect on His Grace generally even in your life, you will come to the conclusion that the sovereignty and supremacy of God is always present. He alone has the authority and the ability to show up in the middle of the storms of your life, whatever they might be, to speak and order calm and restoration like He did for Naomi and me. God alone has the master key into all of our lives to enter when invited, even when we lock ourselves in. It takes that level of power and authority to be God, and there is no one else like Him anywhere.

How to Deliberately Experience God's Grace

3

I f you've learned anything from this discourse so far, it should be that the Grace of God can be experienced by anyone and at any time, solely at the discretion of God Himself. This means that God can decide to shine His Grace on a Hindu, a Muslim, an atheist, a convict or anyone else He chooses. You don't have to be a person who has invited Jesus into their life to be Lord and Saviour in order to experience the benevolence of God's Grace. I hope this doesn't come as a shock to you, if you are a serious Christian.

There are many persons out there who did not grow up in devoted Christian families. Just like me, many of those persons may have come to know Jesus personally only recently. Yet, also like me, many of them can attest to the fact that long before encountering forgiveness and love in Jesus Christ, they experienced many instances of divine intervention in their circumstances. I personally recall numerous instances when I should have been either badly hurt or dead and times when I did things that I should have gone to jail for but for the happening of a miracle that changed the outcomes. Here again you encounter the fact that no one can determine, predict or control when and where God's saving Grace shows up. However, you can thank Him, even right now, that He did show up in your life when you were at your worst and least expected Him to!

Remember that God knows your life from the beginning to the end. I'm convinced that if He brought you out of a bad situation even once in your past, it was because He had a special plan for your life. Otherwise, what would be the point of saving you? He must have had a special assignment for you. Therefore if you're not doing anything to serve God in appreciation for all that He has already done for you, you'd better start doing some serious thinking.

The preceding paragraphs illustrate the ubiquitous and unpredictable nature of God's Grace. They should also serve to reiterate the fact that everyone can experience it but no one can qualify for it. However, there is a way to deliberately stay in the presence of God's Grace so that it ceases to be just an experience in your life, occurring here and there without ownership on your part. There is a way to claim entitlement to the victory and the provision and the mercy and the protection and all the other abundant blessings that come with God's Grace. I alluded to it before. The key is to surrender to God and to hand over your life to Him so that He controls everything that concerns you. Where He goes, you go, and therefore you literally reside under His shadow.

I know that's a mouthful first of all, and secondly, to some it seems utterly unimaginable. How does anyone simply just turn it all over to God? How do you go about it?

The key is to realize first of all that when God made you He had already known the fact that you would be separated from Him because of the sin of Adam that you and I inherited at birth. Armed with this knowledge, God went ahead to design the greatest search-and-rescue mission of all time that would be executed when the time was right in the future. The goal of the search-and-rescue mission was to redeem you and me from the sin we inherited at birth. Finally the time came, over two thousand years ago, and the Trinity deployed Jesus down to the earth in human embodiment to seek and to save God's people who were lost because of the sin they inherited. This is the real beauty in the entire strategy: God gave each and every human being He created a passageway to Jesus so that when Jesus arrived on earth and had successfully executed the plan for our reconciliation and then beckoned us to come freely to Him to receive it, we would be able to. That passageway is called faith, and every single human being God has ever created is a recipient of a measure of it according to the apostle Paul in Romans: *"As God has dealt to each one a measure of faith"* (12:3, NKJV).

Therefore lets look at this thing called faith that enables an ordinary person like you and me to bypass the unpredictability of the manifestation of God's Grace and instead to experience it perpetually and deliberately as a staple in our lives.

WHAT IS FAITH?

These are the top two definitions from the Oxford English Dictionary:

1. Complete trust or confidence in someone or something

2. Strong belief in the doctrines of a religion, based on spiritual conviction rather than proof

The Bible approaches the definition of faith from a curiously different angle. It teaches that faith is a substance, and is yet invisible: *"Now faith is the substance of things hoped for, the evidence of things not seen. For by it the elders obtained a good testimony. By faith we understand that the worlds were framed by the word of God, so that the things which are seen were not made of things which are visible"* (Hebrews 11:1-3, NKJV).

Traditionally we think of a substance as something tangible, something with physical attributes like shape and size, even if only microscopic. But a substance can also mean the subject matter of our deliberations, that is, the things we think about. I find it interesting that faith has both material and spiritual elements in its definition, and not in the sense that you can use one as a metaphor to describe the other, but each element is independent and complete in its own right. When you combine both elements of the definition—that is, the material and the spiritual—the picture that emerges is one in which you can think about your faith, and at the same time you can hold on to it. If you choose to point your faith towards God, then you can anchor yourself to your faith in God even as you reflect on Him.

Faith is a device that God implanted in the thought processes of every single human being He created, which enables a person to innately desire continuity of their daily lives even though they have no material guarantee that tomorrow will exist for them.

You cannot do anything without faith. Faith is hope. Faith is expectation. Faith is action in the direction of your hope and of your expectation. That is why God gives a measure of faith to everyone He creates. You live by your expectations, your hopes and therefore your faith. If you have no hope, expectation or faith in your life, you *will* die. Your faith is connected to God by default because God is our ultimate hope and expectation. Your faith is the substance that draws life from God even when you refuse to acknowledge Him in your life. That is the way God designed it, so that when Jesus beckons you can simply walk on your faith and across to Him. Therefore you cannot live without faith, because you become separated from your life-source and you die. It is that simple. When anyone commits suicide it is because they have become disconnected from their source of life for one reason or other. They cease to see any hope and fail to have any expectation in their lives. The result is a void that is spiritually unbearable, and hence the overwhelming desire to end it all by death.

Those people who remain alive even though they have refused to acknowledge God in their lives do so simply because of the Grace of God. The reason God extends to them this Grace is to give them the opportunity to someday turn their lives over to Him so that they will not ultimately perish. The Bible states in Matthew that God does not wish that any of us, His sheep, should be lost or perish. His desire for everyone is to become reconciled to Him once again in spirit just like it used to be in the beginning when He and Adam used to fellowship in the cool of the morning in the Garden of Eden.

In conclusion, therefore, every human being God creates is given faith, which is the ability to hope, to expect and to believe that your hopes will materialize. You stay alive by the Grace of God, to allow you the opportunity to invite Him into your life one day. If your faith ever departs from you, you immediately seek death because the torture in a faithless life is spiritually unbearable. You can remain alive and have faith but decide to point your faith towards other things, such as New Ageism or some other schism. However, when you do that you declare to God your Maker that you have chosen to divorce Him, and so you leave it up to Him to continue chasing after you, which He will do for a long time, but not forever.

On the other hand, when you decide to point your faith, your hope and your expectations in God's direction and you ask Him into your life to be your Saviour and your Lord, then everything that He owns, which is everything, become yours. You become His child at that point, and not just one of His creations. You become a follower of Christ because God sent Jesus Christ down to earth in human embodiment and asked that we should believe in Him. God asked that we should trust in Jesus because when we trust, we place ourselves in a position where we *must* utilize our faith, our hope and our expectation. We become reliant on Jesus to watch over our affairs, to fight our battles for us and to be our source and sustainer. The sum total of all these are that you surrender completely to God, and then He becomes your Father and you become His child.

The problem most Christians have from here is exercising the authority that comes with being a child of God. That happens because of a lack of knowledge and understanding. That is why the Bible says: "*My people are destroyed for lack of knowledge*" (Hosea 4:6, NKJV).

Many children of God know Him as their Father but don't know their entitlement to His Grace. If you don't know God as your Father you can change that immediately. You can invite Him into your life today to be your Saviour and your Lord. You can give yourself full-time access to His amazing Grace and become a benefactor of His benevolence and His unending love.

The underlying question continues to be "How?" This question, together with the others I've previously posed, are intended to drive this discourse deeper and deeper until we're left with nothing but one of either reaffirmation of your understanding of God's Grace or a decision on your part to deliberately and continually partake of that Grace.

Deciding to Know God

———————— 4 ————————

Most people fail to take the time to learn anything new in their lives, so they allow their minds to be guided by other peoples' thinking. The media tells them what clothes to wear, what foods to eat, what kinds of cars to drive, and even what to believe in. What those people forget to realize is that the media is in the business of making money by any means they can, even if it means selling incorrect information.

I remember watching an infomercial with my wife many years ago which promoted a "revolutionary" hair management product for black hair. This product was supposed to be so amazing that you could eat it and not get hurt. And yet when you were done using it to treat your hair, you would have the best results you ever encountered in a hair treatment product. I don't know what your racial background is, but if you've ever used some of the black hair management products like I used to when jerry curls for men were in vogue, then you know that stuff burns! I used to have to endure painful scabs on my scalp that lasted a whole week sometimes. Therefore watching that infomercial, and seeing the host dip his finger into and eat from the very same container from which he applied product into the hair of the models, was fascinating. We were in awe because now "beauty" would come without pain.

That state of awe didn't last very long however, because months later the very models that were "mmhhing" and "ahhing" on multiple nationally broadcast television stations were suing the product manufacturer because they had all lost their hair! The point to note here is that no one cared to verify the claims of the product manufacturer before allowing them to misinform hordes of innocent consumers and to steal from them in the process. The media raked in millions by selling advertising air time, while the product manufacturer raked in millions by selling a bogus claim on respected national broadcasters' television platforms.

You have to put yourself in a position where you can discern truth from lies; otherwise you become a pawn in a global warfare for power and property that is propelled and compelled by greed, and you wouldn't even know it.

Everything you do starts with a decision. The first major decision you need to make as an intelligent person is to be selective with the information you accept as true in your life.

The second decision is a very close relative of the first, and it is to be selective with the source you rely on for your information. You have to ask yourself these three questions:

1. What does the source of this information stand to gain by pushing this information to me?
2. What do I stand to gain or lose by accepting this information?
3. What is the proof that this information is accurate?

If you fail to go through this brief exercise you are in essence handing over your God-given right to think to whoever the provider of your information is. You don't necessarily want to go through the full exercise with everything you encounter because that will make everyday living rather cumbersome, but you want to be wise and utilize even a miniature version of the exercise for most things. Certainly for major pieces of information or subjects such as those pertaining to what you believe in, you must go through the full exercise.

In my opinion the most important subjects in your life are those pertaining to:

Who you really are
What your purpose on earth is, and
What will happen to you after you die.

SO, WHO ARE YOU REALLY?

In order for me to answer this question, I must first tell you who you are *not* so that we can get that out of the way. Knowing who you're not also makes a good canvas on which to paint the masterpiece of who you are. My hope as well is that in clearly delineating who you are not, we can erase, at least theoretically, some of the baggage that you attach to your identity, which for some has chained them in a place of bondage for decades, like my wife experienced in her life for over 30 years. A few traumatic events in my wife's childhood years were left unaddressed, and they snowballed into a mountain of anxiety that defined most of her life until the bondage-breaking Word of God came in and began to slowly melt away the weight of anxiety that had nearly squeezed all life out of her.

It is very important to note that some of the baggage may not have the outward appearance of something bad. As a matter of fact, some of it might look pretty good, such as great wealth for instance, but can entrap and control your life to the very point of death. This then is a very succinct list of who you are not.

You are not:

The owner of yourself
An afterthought

Anyone's property
A victim of your circumstances
Your race or gender
Your education
Your job title

No matter what anyone says about you, there is only one place on earth that you can trust to define to you who you really are. That place is the Bible.

Since *Deciding to Know God in a Deeper Way* is not an attempt to argue against the numerous ridiculous proposals that try to tell you that you were once a tadpole or a baboon, or that there was once a cosmic accident out of which derived such order and precision in the world that even the fields of science and engineering are yet to completely fathom, I will stay focused on the final authority of the world, which is the Word of God, encapsulated in the Bible. This, therefore, is who the Bible declares you to be:

1. You are a deliberate and calculated creation of God.
2. You were designed to rule and to reign over every other thing God ever created.
3. You are destined to regain your original authority over everything created.

You are not the guest who showed up at a party and found that he had not been accounted for, so the host had to hurriedly set a place in order to accommodate him. You are not the man who intended to drive to one part of town but got lost along the way and arrived someplace else he was not supposed to be. God designed you with purpose; He knows you by name and is interested in everything that concerns you. You may be nodding your head right now and saying "That's right!" or you may be wondering:

If He knows you by name, then where has He been all these years,

When your husband or wife left you with mountains of
bills and a broken heart?
When the love of your life died and left you alone in this
world?
When your children turned their backs on you and cursed
you on top of it?
When the bank kicked you to the curb because you could
no longer pay the mortgage?
When the doctor handed you the diagnosis from hell?

Where is He even now, when everything in your life seems to be
falling apart?
What kind of God just sits idly by and watches the people He loves
go through one calamity after the other?

If you're asking even one of these questions, then you're in
good company, because I asked them all, and even some I don't dare
write on paper anymore. There are even millions of Christians today
who have known God for many years but are still struggling with
these very same questions.

I remember counselling a wonderful Christian lady recently
who was a regular viewer of *Nite Lite Live*, the call-in TV show I
hosted several times a month on CTS Television. Her husband had
just filed for divorce after over 30 years of marriage, and all her children had turned their backs on her and wouldn't even take her
phone calls. Their father had poisoned their minds against her. This
dear lady is in her retirement years and has no connection with the
closest people she knows in the world. The man she stuck with in
spite of many years of abuse and the children she bore from her own
womb and nurtured through incredibly hard times all alone had all
written her off at the time in her life when she needed them most.

So you may be asking the question, "Where is God in this
sweet lady's situation?" This doesn't quite sound like the life of a
person who was deliberately and precisely made. It certainly doesn't

sound like the life of a person who should be ruling over anything in the world. If these are your conclusions, then you were right the first time and you are right the second time.

WHAT IS YOUR PURPOSE IN LIFE?

However, there is a piece missing from the above picture. The piece is God, the Almighty Creator of everything in the world. If you understand Him, then the picture above changes dramatically and makes complete sense. You see, God made you and me for His purpose. That purpose is multifaceted and in fact includes the mandate for humanity to rule and to reign over everything He created. He made us to be stewards of His Kingdom, but with the rights of sons and daughters.

Who you are makes absolutely no sense until you know your purpose on earth. Your purpose is not to become the CEO of a multinational company. Your purpose is not to become an Olympic gold medalist. Your purpose is not to be a great mother. Your purpose is not to be a great pastor even. If you take away the purpose of God from all of these great aspirations, it boils down to nothing, because when death arrives it renders your personal purpose meaningless. Without the purpose of God ruling your life, neither your obstacles nor your achievements make any sense.

Why would any intelligent person want to live if cars, houses, vacations, jewellery and a large bank account were all that life offered? I've known wealthy friends who lay down in their beds of sickness, incapable of enjoying any of the good things their money afforded them. If you asked any one of them to trade you their fortune for your good health, they'd gladly do it. Yet people, even some Christians, place such a high value on material things that these things become idols of worship in their lives.

When you don't understand the purpose of God for your life you equate to a robot, merely responding to instructions until the day your engine shuts down. But when you understand that God wants you to be the CEO of a multinational corporation so that you can help to propagate His agenda in the world, and when you understand that by winning an Olympic gold medal you will gain a platform that will allow God to use you to further the preaching of His gospel to the world, the picture begins to look different, because God's purpose for your life is the climax of every other purpose in your life.

When your alarm comes alive in the morning, for most people its purpose is to wake them up from sleep. Then the purpose for waking up from sleep takes over, which might be to get to work on time. Of course, the purposes for which you work would be manifold, but largely it is to take care of yourself and perhaps your family. These small purposes all lead up to larger and larger ones, which without the climax of fulfilling God's purpose for your life becomes like a great movie script that has no ending. It can't make much sense. Imagine a protagonist in a movie who goes through all kinds of trials and upheavals in his or her life and remains hopeful and tenacious, but then the movie ends abruptly. It leaves you, the viewer, feeling frustrated and wishing perhaps that you had invested your time into some other endeavour that would have been more fulfilling and meaningful.

In Genesis, the story is told of Joseph, the beloved son of Jacob, whose brothers sold him to Ishmaelite traders on their way to Egypt because they were jealous of him and wanted to get rid of him. Jacob, their father, loved Joseph dearly, and that made some of his other sons unhappy, so when they got the opportunity to get rid of their brother they seized it. Joseph was only a teenager when his brothers conspired against him. First he was thrown into a dark pit, and then they pulled him out and sold him to slave traders. To explain to their father why he didn't return home with them that night, his brothers concocted a story that he'd been devoured by a wild animal.

Imagine just for a moment what was going through the young

Joseph's mind as his brothers whom he grew up with and loved and with whom he played and got into trouble seized him forcefully and hauled him into a dark, cold pit. He might have thought they were playing at first, perhaps as wildly as they had many times in the past. The Bible doesn't say exactly how long they left him in the dark pit, but it was for a while because they had time to eat a meal and discuss amongst themselves what to do with him. You can almost hear him calling out with increasing desperation, "Let me out, guys. Let me out!" Then when they did eventually let him out, it wasn't to say to him "Gotcha!" but it was to hand him over to complete strangers in exchange for some money.

By now he must have started feeling really desperate and was maybe even beginning to ask for his father. And then as the strange men tied him up and hauled him onto the back of one of their camels as though he was a roll of rugs going to market, he must have been crying, perhaps apologizing to his brothers for things he couldn't even remember doing wrong. He must have been promising them he would never hurt any of them again or say anything bad to any of them.

But then they looked smaller and smaller in the distance as the camels slowly but steadily headed onwards in the direction of Egypt. They couldn't hear him anymore. His pleas had gone unanswered. The anguish in his heart must have been choking him like a noose around his neck. What had he done to deserve this? How could his own brothers do such a thing to him? How could the God of his father, grandfather and great-grandfather allow such a thing to happen to him? You have to agree with me that none of it would have made any sense to young Joseph.

This story would have been as tragic as any story could ever be, were it not for the fact that God was present within the details of its unravelling. God was completely aware of all that was going on and had already determined to use it to glorify His name. When you are trapped in what seems like the valley of the shadow of death, and it seems like all hell has broken loose around you, and you can't see any way out of your situation, God is there with you, even when you don't feel that way. This may shock many Christians, but even if you are not a believer in Jesus, He is there for you when calamity overtakes you. That is the awesomeness of His Grace! He may or may not thwart the attack on your life if you are not His follower, but He knows exactly what you're going through. Like I've mentioned before, however, the one sure way to have Him intercede on your behalf every time is to surrender your life to Him. When you do that, you know for sure that He will never leave you alone in your difficulties.

This is a brief look into the life of Joseph in Egypt, after his brothers had sold him into slavery:

> *Now Joseph had been taken down to Egypt; And Potiphar, an officer of Pharaoh, captain of the guard, an Egyptian, bought him from the Ishmaelites who had taken him down there. The LORD was with Joseph, and he was a successful man; and he was in the house of his master the Egyptian. And his master saw that the LORD was with him and that the LORD made all he did to prosper in his hand. So Joseph found favor in his sight, and served him. Then he made him overseer of his house, and all that he had he put under his authority. So it was, from the time that he had made him overseer of his house and all that he had, that the LORD blessed the Egyptian's house for Joseph's sake; and the blessing of the LORD was on all that he had in the house and in the field. Thus he left all that he had in Joseph's hand, and he did not know what he had except for the bread which he ate.* (Genesis 39:1-6, NKJV)

Remember, I mentioned previously that the obstacles and the victories in your life have no meaning until God becomes the focus of your life. You could be ravaged by difficulties or flooded by financial abundance; without God both extremes of suffering and abundance are pointless, because when death comes nothing matters anymore. I assure you, however, that if you allow God into your life to save your soul and then go as far as asking Him to use you to propagate His divine purpose in this world, He will reward you, because that's the promise He makes in Matthew:

Therefore do not worry, saying, "What shall we eat?" or "What shall we drink?" or "What shall we wear?" For after all these things the Gentiles seek. For your heavenly Father knows that you need all these things. But seek first the kingdom of God and His righteousness, and all these things shall be added to you. (6:31-33, NKJV)

As desperate as the situation of the lady who contacted me through the TV show is, if she stays connected to God by faith and is willing to be used by God for His purpose, goodness will emanate from the mess in her life, and victory will be the conclusion of her life story.

God created you and me for His purpose. When you place your purpose ahead of God's your life ends up meaningless; your successes and your failures make no sense. And the ultimate loss for anyone who shuts God out of their lives is that the original destiny that He designed for humankind according to Genesis 1 is not experienced:

Then God said, "Let Us make man in Our image, according to Our likeness; let them have dominion over the fish of the sea, over the birds of the air, and over the cattle, over all the earth and over every creeping thing that creeps on the earth." So God created man in His own image; in the image of God He created him; male and female He created them. Then God blessed them, and God said to them, "Be fruitful and multiply; fill the earth and subdue it; have dominion over the fish of the sea, over the birds of the air, and over every living thing that moves on the earth." (26-28, NKJV)

When you look around your environment you see purpose in nature, not a succession of glorious accidents. The moment a tiny single seed is sown into the ground, it is purposed by its very DNA to grow into a plant. This plant is useful in some way or the other, either as food, medicine, or a thing of beauty and ultimately as a source of oxygen. All of creation would be defunct without the oxygen produced by the purpose written into the DNA of that little seed.

WHAT HAPPENS TO YOU WHEN YOU DIE?

If missing out on the dominion experience described previously was all there was to it, you could feel sorry for those who would make the mistake of not experiencing it and that would be the end of it. However, it gets worse and never gets better; if you haven't made the decision to know God in a personal relationship so that He can save your soul and be your life-guide, the end game is a life in hell for the rest of eternity. God promises that conclusion, and that is why He goes into such incredible lengths to draw you close to Him. You wouldn't want your children winding up on death row, so you do everything in your power to teach them the right things. However, at the end of the day we each have the prerogative of choice, and the decision we make has everlasting consequences. You must choose wisely, because just like heaven is a real place, so is hell.

MY TESTIMONY

Don't make the mistake I made for many years. In my heart I knew there had to be a creator of the world because there can be no perpetual order in randomness. Things couldn't have just "fallen into place." The sun cannot rise predictably for thousands of years and set at its appointed time every single day without interruption simply by a freak accident at some point in the timeline of the universe. The moon takes up the night shift like clockwork day in and day out without human prompting, while affecting the flow of the world's oceans, weather patterns, vegetation and all the elements of nature that combine in perfect harmony to sustain life. That *cannot* happen by accident.

But even though I thought through this regularly and sought to find the one who designed and orchestrated such an unmatchable enterprise, my search took me to all the wrong places. I talked to many people but never got any answers that made any sense to me. I read dozens and dozens of books on the religions of the world, psychology and philosophy, but always came up short; there was always something missing. I wanted answers and not a preacher in a suit yelling at me about some guy named Jesus who died on the cross for my sins. If He couldn't help Himself on the cross, how could He help me? How could God allow Himself to be beaten and bruised and left to die on a cross? How dumb could some people be, believing all that rubbish? I nearly drove myself crazy asking all those questions and never getting any real answers.

So after over twenty years of asking those questions and not getting any answers that made sense to me, I resorted to take matters in my own hands; I wrote a book I called *Reconstructing God.* The subtitle of the book was *Proposals Toward an Optimum Humanity.* In that book I proposed that God did not exist, and I attempted to formulate a new concept of God that I believed would be more useful to humanity—a more efficient god, as I put it at the time. When the book was published, I was invited by the Learning Annex to offer seminars based on the contents of the book. I had used some of the concepts from the book to create groundwork for a brand new religion, which I called "deitology."

In spite of the fact that I'd attended a Catholic boarding school and had access to the Bible, I looked everywhere for information except the one place where I should've been looking for it—the Bible. Shortly after *Reconstructing God* was published I sent a copy to some relatives in Texas and Louisiana in the United States, to announce my proud achievement. Unknown to me they were staunch followers of Jesus, which was a surprise to me because I knew the colourful lives some of them used to live.

With inspired tenacity they prayed and fasted for me for nearly two years until the day the Grace of God arrested me on the streets of Houston, Texas, as I drove my SUV on my way home to my brother's house, where I lived at the time. That was the day I had my first real encounter with God, and since then my life has not been the same. Today I testify about the God whom I once cursed. I do this because of the personal encounter I had with Him, which changed my life forever. That encounter gave me a new revelation of who He really is and the depths of what He did for you and me over 2000 years ago.

GOD DESIRES YOUR LOVE

Since the experience I had with God in Houston I have continually studied to learn more about Him. I have learned that there is archaeological evidence that Jesus, the son of God, actually walked the face of the earth, contrary to my old, uneducated conclusion in my ignorant days. He was indeed born of a virgin mother and grew up in Israel. He worked as a carpenter until He began His ministry of reconciliation at the age of thirty. That was the reason He had come down to the earth, to become the bridge between God and the people God had created but had become permanently separated from Him because of sin. Jesus substituted Himself in our place because you and I were separated from God at birth because of the sins of our pedigree. By taking our sins onto Himself and by allowing Himself to be judged, condemned and hung to die, Jesus paid the price in full for you and me to be reconciled once again to our Maker and to become partakers of His kingdom. This is how John 3:16 puts it: *"For God so loved the world that He gave His only begotten Son, that whoever believes in Him should not perish but have everlasting life"* (NKJV).

God never asked us to *obey* Jesus in order to be saved. Rather, He admonished *all* of humanity to *believe* in Him, to *trust* Him, in order to be saved and be reconciled. The reason for God desiring our trust instead of our obedience in order to be reconciled to Him is really very simple.

The foundation of obedience is rooted in the most basic aspects of your cognitive architecture. That's why chickens can be taught to become obedient. It is basic and is a close relative of the instinct to survive, which is available to all animals. Hence you can obey just to avoid the pain of punishment that would otherwise by inflicted. Obedience requires you to do something to please God, which is well and good, except for the fact that Satan too does things to please God; therefore obedience is nothing really special. In Job when God gave Satan permission to interfere in Job's life and to inflict him with calamity to test his faith, God gave Satan a clear order not to tamper with Job's life. In order to please God and avoid God's wrath, Satan obeyed. Yet Satan hates God.

God desires your unconditional love. In fact, He demands it in the same way that you would from the ones you love. How would you feel if your husband or wife married you out of obedience to his or her parents instead of a deep and unconditional love for you? When you love someone, you offer yourself to them. God requires nothing less than that from you and me. When you believe in Jesus and trust Him to be your Lord and Saviour, you are in effect saying to Him, "I love You back, and I appreciate what You've done for me," because it was out of the abundance of God's unconditional love for you and me that He sent Jesus to die on the cross. Jesus accepted this unfathomable task in spite of the tremendous pain it entailed. That is the stuff unconditional love—God style—is made of. The key to enter deliberately into the gates of His Grace is through your total surrender to Him. This is only possible by trusting and believing in Him *completely.* You can obey without any faith at all, but you cannot trust and believe, even a little bit, without faith.

Deciding to Know God in a Deeper Way

I have shared with you what Jesus has done in my life. All you have to do is tune your television to a Christian channel such as *CTS,* where I hosted *Nite Lite Live,* or *TBN* or perhaps *The Word Network* and many others to see the millions of people who have found Him demonstrate their love for Him and their worship of Him. All you have to do is visit a well grounded Christian church and witness how passionately people just like yourself pursue a relationship with Jesus. Amongst these people are engineers, doctors, stockbrokers, nurses, company CEOs, bank presidents, professors, millionaires, billionaires, inventors, young and old people from all backgrounds and from every corner of the world! Listen to their testimonies of how Jesus came into their lives and changed everything.

Now I know you're smart; otherwise you wouldn't be reading a book with a title like *Deciding to Know God in a Deeper Way.* However, in spite of your level of intelligence, and perhaps even your academic prowess, you are definitely not smarter than all those people, millions of them around the world, who have surrendered their lives to and live for Jesus.

On the flip side are other people formerly hooked on drugs, those who used to be hooked on pornography, former child molesters, ex-bank robbers, convicted murderers, and the list goes on and on. When Jesus offered Himself as a sacrifice to God on the cross over 2000 years ago in Israel, He took away the sins of those people too! He substituted Himself for them and took upon Him the spiritual judgments that they should've been responsible for. In the process He gave them a brand new start for the rest of their lives.

I like this analogy: How do you feel when you see the ones you love, especially your children, struggling with life? How do you feel as a parent, or brother or sister, when the ones you love deeply and dearly are struggling with an illness? Do you sometimes wish you could suffer in their place, that somehow you could endure it better than they can? When you see those you love, like a child no longer living at home, struggling financially, don't you step in if you can?

How do you feel when your child, or those you love dearly, has their heart broken in a relationship that has gone wrong? Don't you just feel like getting right into the middle of it to make it all better?

Jesus asks those who choose to trust Him to lay all their burdens on Him. Then He goes further to promise rest, peace, guidance and sustenance. He says that it doesn't matter what you've done wrong; if you say and are truly sorry for those things, He forgives you completely right now! That is the meaning of His Grace. If you've cheated on your spouse; if you've abandoned your children; if you've stolen from your boss; if you ran someone over and took off without stopping to help; whether you raped someone, even your own child—it doesn't matter what you've done. If you apologize to Him with humility and sincerity, then He forgives you immediately. That is the Grace of God, and there is nothing you can do to earn it, and nothing you can do to lose it as long as you stay surrendered to Jesus.

He could have called in an army of angels to destroy His enemies if He had wanted to as He hung on the cross to die for you and me. He could have inspired His followers to fight for His life if He had wanted to. He could have simply vanished or prevented His death by one of many ways. But the sole reason He came down from heaven and went through all that He went through was because there was no other way for Him to legally redeem you and me from our sinful inheritance except to take on our sins, be judged for them, and be condemned for them so that the sentence would have been served and the price for our freedom would have been fully settled. That is an unusual kind of love.

If you pause for a moment to think about it, allowing Himself to be crucified for our sins was the surest way to make you ask yourself this question: "If He went as far as to die for me, what is there He wouldn't do for me?"

Keep in mind that He knew that He would be raised because of His sinless nature and His godliness. Your country's president doesn't have that power and will not offer his life in exchange for yours. The prime minister of your country, your senator, governor and even your pastor will not lay down their lives in exchange for yours! There are even many parents who will not lay down their lives in exchange for the lives of their own children. But Jesus gave up His life for you so that a bridge of reconciliation would be built between you and God. Now all you have to do is walk on the platform of your faith and across that bridge, which is Jesus, and back home to your Father, who is the Creator of everything in the world. Tell Him you love Him and that you trust Him, because His will for your life is by far better than anything you've ever imagined for yourself.

You see, knowing God in a personal relationship is a decision you have to make. He has always been there, inviting you to *allow* Him to come into your life. But when He made you, He gave you the free will to choose and do with your life as you please. The way that you want to be loved and cherished just for who you are is the same way that He wants to be loved and cherished just for who He is. He doesn't want to manipulate you. He doesn't want to force you. He doesn't want to play cheap tricks and gimmicks to win you over.

Even if you're upset with Him for any reason, turn your life to Him and let Him know that you're mad at Him for whatever reason. He will comfort you and reveal things to you about your life and circumstances that will amaze you. Just ask those who have turned their lives over to Him. I am one of them. And because I surrendered my life completely to Him, I am now a constant partaker of His supernatural gift of Grace every single day of my life.

REVIEW SUMMARY

1. The Grace of God is His unmatchable supernatural ability and capacity to interject Himself into the life of anyone He chooses and at anytime He chooses in order to bless them in one way or other.

2. No human being can qualify themselves to merit this incredible gift from God called His Grace.

3. Yet every human being can be a beneficiary of this benevolence of God.

4. Even though no human being qualifies for God's Grace, every human being can deliberately set themselves up so that the Grace of God can become a perpetual part of their daily experience.

5. The key is faith in the Lord Jesus Christ.

6. Everyone has *essential* faith, but everyone must each make a personal decision to invest their faith in Jesus, as opposed to someone or something else, such as a bogus saviour or New Ageism for instance.

RATIONAL FOUNDATION FOR SEEKING GOD

5

Genesis 1:3-25 tells the story of how God created the rest of the world. In verse 26 God created His masterpiece, our human pedigree. This is the account of that awesome event: *"Then God said, 'Let Us make man in Our image, according to Our likeness; let them have dominion over the fish of the sea, over the birds of the air, and over the cattle, over all the earth and over every creeping thing that creeps on the earth'"* (Genesis 1:26, NKJV).

The God who created the world is one God, but He has three parts, God the Father, God the Son and God the Holy Spirit. When He made humankind in His image, therefore, He made us with three parts to our persons: a physical body, a soul and a spirit.

Your soul, which is the hub of your rationality, is made up of your mind, your will and your emotions and resembles God the Father, who decrees all things. Your thinking and decision-making are done through your soul, which in essence directs your life the same way God the Father directs the world.

Your body, which the Bible exhorts you to present to God as a living sacrifice, symbolizes Jesus the Son, who came down to the earth in human embodiment to offer Himself as a living sacrifice in order to execute the divine search-and-rescue mission devised in heaven to buy back a humanity that had been sold to Satan through Adam's sin.

Your spirit resembles the Holy Spirit, whom the Bible says witnesses to *our* spirits when we accept Jesus' Lordship over our lives.

Our focus in this portion of the discourse is your soul, the hub of all your decision-making activities and epicentre of your thinking. It's been said that the greatest battle in the world has been fought for thousands of years, and every human being has participated in every generation. That is because that battle is not a geopolitical battle between nations, groups or individuals but is between the two ears on the head of every person; it is in your thinking, in your mind. Whoever succeeds in influencing your thinking enlists you as a soldier in their army.

When God spoke to the people of Israel through the prophet Isaiah saying, *"Come now, and let us reason together"* (1:18, NKJV), He was appealing to their minds and their thinking because He wanted them to *understand* what He had to say to them. This is what He said:

> *"Though your sins are like scarlet, They shall be as white as snow; Though they are red like crimson, They shall be as wool. If you are willing and obedient, You shall eat the good of the land; But if you refuse and rebel, You shall be devoured by the sword";* for the mouth of the LORD has spoken. (Isaiah 1:18-20, NKJV)

God desired for them to understand what He was saying to them; however *He* was in charge and therefore dictated the terms of the conversation. He wasn't arguing with the people but was making them a solemn promise to bless them on the condition that they would be obedient. Each person therefore had the opportunity to think through God's rational offer and to make up their minds to accept or reject it while understanding the consequences of their decision.

Your decisions dictate your actions, and your actions drive your destiny. Proverbs 23:7 says that as a man *"thinks in his heart, so is he"* (NKJV). Therefore when Satan throws calamities of all kinds at you, his desire is not to hurt your body but to conquer your mind. If he does enough to take your mind off of the things of God so that you literarily *meditate* on your misfortunes, then he has your mind exactly where he wants it. While God is in charge of the world, *you* are in charge of your mind; therefore you have the power to dictate the terms of your thinking.

The seventeenth century French theo-philosopher Blaise Pascal made a remarkable logical argument in his posthumously published work entitled *Pensées,* which means "Thoughts" in English. This work was by all accounts his life's crowning jewel and has been extremely influential in Christian apologetics. In it he talked about the "wager" and offered the following argument, which I will loosely paraphrase for simplicity:

Assume that you had only two choices in life: to believe in the existence of God and follow Him, or be an atheist and not believe in God. A person with a sound mind who has only basic knowledge of the promises of God and the emptiness and futility in atheism, even with no proof, will choose God. This is why: The chances of dying and going up to heaven to be with God or becoming a meaningless corpse if there is nothing after death is 50/50, since you have only two choices. You can bet either way.

If you placed your bet on atheism and you won, you would actually have gained nothing because there would be nothing to gain; after death you become a thread in history and that's it. On the other hand, if you wagered on God and all His promises and you won, you would have heaven, all its promises and Jesus Christ after you died.

But then the argument gets really good; if it turned

out that you were right in being an atheist, meaning that there was really nothing after death, then you would have lost everything anyway, because there was never anything to gain in the first place.

But let's assume that you had placed your bet on God and it turned out that you were right; the picture would look completely different. First off, you would have the promises of God, and the fellows who placed their bets on atheism would've been snookered. The reason would be that if God exists, then so must hell, and there is in fact no place for atheism. He would have lost out on the benefits of being in heaven, but now he would have to deal with hell for the rest of time.

Either way, therefore, you are better off betting on God. If you lose the bet on God because He doesn't exist, it is equivalent to winning the bet on atheism, because you gain nothing anyway. But if you win the bet on God the picture is completely different. Therefore betting on God is the only rational decision to make, because it *always* gives you a chance.

BUILDING YOUR FAITH RATIONALLY

We're continuing to drill down this discourse. We started from the point of the question of the Grace of God, down to its many manifestations, further down to how to appropriate it permanently by making a decision to know God, and now we're at the level of establishing some important truths in your thinking.

This is important because your mind is the gateway into your spirit. That is why God requires your permission to establish His Lordship in your life. *You* have to make a decision for Him to come into your life; otherwise He may just leave you well alone. You have to put your faith to its ultimate use, which is to heed the call of God to allow Him to be your Saviour and Guide. To do this you have to invest that tiny mustard seed of faith that God wrote into your DNA. You make that investment of faith nowhere else but in God Himself.

By virtue of God's sovereignty and His Grace, He can choose to bestow supernatural faith in anyone and at anytime. What I've written about so far has been on *essential* faith, which everyone has and without which death is the immediate choice. Supernatural faith, on the other hand, is a special gift from God, which He chooses to dispense in the same way that He does other special gifts, such as great oratory prowess and athleticism. And since you don't know the mind of God and exactly how He plans to execute the details of His grand plan, you cannot just allow the mustard-seed-size faith that He gave you to just remain small. He gave you faith so that you would seek Him first in your life and then go on and live a life of faith and hopefulness. You *must* therefore make good use of what He has already given you, so that you may demonstrate your good stewardship and diligence. Yes, it is important to guard your faith and be careful about where you direct it.

In Matthew Jesus taught the importance of good stewardship and diligence with the parable of the talents. Pay very close attention to what happened to the servant who decided to do nothing with that which his master gave him to take care of:

> For the kingdom of heaven is like a man traveling to a far country, who called his own servants and delivered his goods to them. And to one he gave five talents, to another two, and to another one, to each according to his own ability; and immediately he went on a journey. Then he who had received the five talents went and traded with them, and made another five talents. And likewise he who had received two gained two more also. But he who had received one went and dug in the ground, and hid his lord's money. After a long time the lord of those servants came and settled accounts with them. So he who had received five talents

came and brought five other talents, saying, "Lord, you delivered to me five talents; look, I have gained five more talents besides them." His lord said to him, "Well done, good and faithful servant; you were faithful over a few things, I will make you ruler over many things. Enter into the joy of your lord." He also who had received two talents came and said, "Lord, you delivered to me two talents; look, I have gained two more talents besides them." His lord said to him, "Well done, good and faithful servant; you have been faithful over a few things, I will make you ruler over many things. Enter into the joy of your lord." Then he who had received the one talent came and said, "Lord, I knew you to be a hard man, reaping where you have not sown, and gathering where you have not scattered seed. And I was afraid, and went and hid your talent in the ground. Look, there you have what is yours." But his lord answered and said to him, "You wicked and lazy servant, you knew that I reap where I have not sown, and gather where I have not scattered seed. So you ought to have deposited my money with the bankers, and at my coming I would have received back my own with interest. So take the talent from him, and give it to him who has ten talents. For to everyone who has, more will be given, and he will have abundance; but from him who does not have, even what he has will be taken away. And cast the unprofitable servant into the outer darkness. There will be weeping and gnashing of teeth." (25:14-30, NKJV)

You may not know this, but the measure of faith God placed in you can actually grow. It can grow in one of two ways, or if you are highly favoured by God your faith can grow both ways. Firstly, it can grow supernaturally by God's Grace, and secondly, you can make a decision to grow it rationally. Since you don't know whether or not God's plan for your life has the gift of supernatural faith included in it, we'll focus in this section on *you* growing your faith rationally, however still by the Grace of God.

A Lesson from Thomas "the Doubter"

When Jesus Christ gave His life on the cross at Calvary in the year AD 32, all the hope His disciples had must have died with Him because they hadn't understood what He meant when He said He would be raised on the third day. Therefore many of them cowered out of sight for fear they might be ostracized on account of their association with Jesus.

One disciple in particular has been dealt a bad reputation by Christians all over the world, to the extent that even secular society has embraced it and incorporated the unfair analysis of his character into their everyday lingo. That disciple is Thomas, whose desire to see Jesus with his own eyes before believing that He had indeed been resurrected has earned him the inglorious title of *Thomas the Doubter.*

I don't know about you, but after such a "catastrophic disappointment" such as the disciples incorrectly perceived, if I were one of them and living under the real threat of death by crucifixion, I would want to see proof before surrendering my faith again. That is the natural working of the God-given human ability to think and reason.

Jesus, who is God, understands our need for proof. So even though He clearly applauds those who believe without the requirement of proof, He also will not discard anyone whose desire for proof is a genuine longing to know the truth about Him. When He rose from death the Bible recounts numerous instances when He presented Himself to His followers *so that they would believe.* He could have appeared to them in visions or sent angels to inform them of His resurrection. But Jesus knew the importance and the necessity of presenting Himself to them in the flesh, so that's what He did.

When He finally appeared to Thomas, in the company of the other disciples to whom He had previously appeared, Jesus did not castigate Thomas. As a matter of fact, He didn't just appear in that meeting but went a step further and invited Thomas to touch the wounds in His hands where He had been nailed to the cross. There again Jesus knew that just showing up wouldn't be good enough to convince the deeply troubled and fear-stricken mind of Thomas and the others. He placed the onus of proof on Himself and followed through with the invitation to His disciples to touch His wounds.

Therefore even though Jesus' disciples believed that He was indeed the Son of God prior to His crucifixion, after He was resurrected and He presented Himself to them their faith in Him became so strong that nearly all of them endured the punishment of death by crucifixion or beheading, *for His sake,* because they knew with absolute certainty that Jesus was who He said He was.

When the emperor Nero, who ruled Rome in AD 64, decided to systematically wipe out all Christians who would not recant their eyewitness testimonies of Jesus' resurrection, 11 of the disciples, including Peter and Paul, were brutally murdered. They died because they knew the truth and would not let that truth go in vain. In fact the story goes that both Peter and Paul requested to be crucified upside down because they did not deem themselves worthy of being crucified in the same way that Jesus was. How powerful!

So by using practical reasoning, like Thomas and the other disciples did and many others have done over the centuries, we acquire knowledge regarding the things of God. Your faith in Him is wonderful, but keep in mind that life happens and sometimes the hand you're dealt can shake the very foundations of your faith, like it did for Jesus' disciples merely days after He died! Those were people who saw Him heal large populations of all kinds of sick persons. They saw Him perform incredible miracles. They witnessed Jesus curse a fruitless tree, which proceeded to wither instantaneously. They even saw Him walk on water! Yet at the first sign of trouble their courage failed.

You need to fortify your mind and your thinking with the kind of information that will settle once and for all the question of who Jesus is, so that when the foundations of your faith are rocked by circumstances in your life and you have to revert to your rational mind, you won't allow the enemy of God to manipulate you like he's done very successfully in the lives of many Christians. The rational here is that you cannot think below or outside the level of your capacity to think. If therefore your mind is saturated with the truth of God and you know categorically who Jesus really is, then even when your faith becomes frail, as it does sometimes, you can only fall down to the level of the truth in your mind, which is the truth of God. Hence it is necessary to build your faith rationally, even as you allow the Spirit of God to increase your faith supernaturally.

These are three very practical things you can do to build your faith rationally this very day:

1. Read your Bible regularly. Romans 10:17 says, *"So then faith comes by hearing, and hearing by the word of God"* (NKJV).
2. Study the history of the church and Christianity in general, and see how it relates to ancient history and modern history and continues to relate to our daily lives.
3. Study the most amazing prophetic verse of the Bible, Daniel 9:25:

Know therefore and understand, That from the going forth of the command To restore and build Jerusalem Until Messiah the Prince, There shall be seven weeks and sixty-two weeks; The street shall be built again, and the wall, Even in troublesome times. (NKJV)

This verse from Daniel is a prophecy given to him by the angel Gabriel, concerning the timing of Jesus' triumphal entry into

Jerusalem. This prophecy was given to Daniel five hundred years before it actually happened! And when it did happen, it happened with mathematical precision, down to the last day.

Jerusalem had been in ruins after three successive sieges by Nebuchadnezzar of Babylon, first as a general in his father's army, and later as king of Babylon. Then Cyrus, a Medo-Persian military genius, defeated Nebuchadnezzar in battle, and the Persian Empire became the dominant player in the world. Babylon ruled the world from 606 BC to 539 BC, and then the Persians ruled from 539 BC to 332 BC. It was during the Persian rule that Artaxerxes Longimanus, then ruler, issued the decree to restore Jerusalem on March 14, 445 BC. You can find the Scripture reference in Nehemiah 2:5-18.

The timeline given by the angel Gabriel's prophecy was *"seven weeks and sixty-two weeks,"* which translates to 173,880 days. To arrive at 173,880 days there are a few things we have to understand about the Hebrew calendar, a subject so big that dozens of books have been written on it. In *Learn the Bible in 24 Hours*, Dr. Chuck Missler explains Daniel 9:25 in detail. Dr. Missler's book is a great resource because it provides readers with solid scientific and practical detail in support of God's sovereignty. However, for the purposes of this book, here's a synopsis of Daniel 9:25.

The Hebrew calendar recognizes the weeks of days, which is actually 7 days; the weeks of weeks, which is 7 weeks; the weeks of months, which is 7 months; and the weeks of years, which is 7 years. The prophecy refers to the weeks of years. Therefore when you add 7 weeks and 62 weeks you get 69 weeks. The Bible recognizes a year as having 360 days. This therefore is the calculation to arrive at 173,880 days: $69 \times 7 \times 360 = 173,880$.

From March 14, 445 BC, when Artaxerxes Longimanus issued the decree to rebuild Jerusalem, to April 6, 32 AD, when Jesus rode the donkey into Jerusalem, it is exactly 173,880 days. Remember that the prophecy was given to Daniel five hundred years before!

That is simply amazing. But then again, we're talking about the one who created the world.

When you take the kinds of practical steps I have suggested, you fortify your rational mind with the truth, thereby planting your mind solidly in God. In Matthew 22:37-38 Jesus teaches, "*You shall love the* LORD *your God with all your heart, with all your soul, and with all your mind.' This is the first and great commandment*" (NKJV).

Again, when you take these practical steps, you position yourself to receive power and revelation from the Holy Spirit that will build your faith, and also you gain important knowledge that will prevent you from blowing about like a leaf in the wind when life happens to you and threatens your faith.

God says in Hosea, "*My people are destroyed for lack of knowledge. Because you have rejected knowledge, I also will reject you from being priest for Me; Because you have forgotten the law of your God, I also will forget your children*" (4:6, NKJV).

I suggest to you that faith that is founded on the Grace of God and supported through practical knowledge is a lasting kind of faith. Human beings have demonstrated their ability to take God's Grace for granted since the beginning of time. In spite of the numerous times that God poured His Grace over the people of Israel, for instance, they never failed to turn their backs on Him again and again and again. That is why it is important to provide some strong intellectual reference points for yourself, so that when everything around you seems to be falling apart you will know that the matter concerning God is settled. You can then focus your attention and strength on calling out to Him to help you, instead of allowing yourself to be buried in doubt and confusion and running the real risk of allowing Satan to brainwash you with lies.

Your faith must be steady and focused and not vacillate with the forever changing opinions of the day. Knowledge has the power to unshackle your mind from the grip of ignorance. Satan thrives on ignorance. That's how he can cause you to perish, by lying to you because you don't know the truth. The worst mistake you can make as a human being is to allow yourself to be fooled right through till you die. Because if you die without activating your faith for God, it is too late and there is no turning back. Jesus says in the book of John, "*And you shall know the truth, and the truth shall make you free*" (John 8:32, NKJV).

YOUR PERSONAL COVENANT WITH GOD

In the opening chapters of this discourse I talked at length about God's invitation to you and me to enter into a unique covenant with Him. I talked about one of the nuances of the covenant being that God, by His Grace, would dictate the terms of the covenant and then absolve you of any performance obligations save the requirement to accept or reject His offer.

In this section the one who orchestrates the covenant with God is you. The terms of the agreement remain the same, but now you're responding to God with an invitation of your own. God still dictates the terms and still absolves you of any performance requirements other than to walk the red carpet of His Grace into relationship with Him. However, keep in mind that when you do enter into this relationship with God, He takes control. If you insist on being the driver in the relationship, God will not fight with you, but things will not go well. I tried doing it my way and failed woefully many times, so I do know what I'm writing about.

I have included the published account of when I tried taking the driver seat in my relationship with God many years ago, long before He revealed Himself to me. This account is taken directly from *Reconstructing God: Proposals Towards an Optimum Humanity* (Sam Tita, Titanium Lyrics Press: 2004), the book that culminated my misguided search for God. This is how far astray one can get when God is not embraced for who He is and is not allowed to direct our lives.

.....

Deciding to Know God in a Deeper Way

June 1992

I gently placed the book I was reading on the desk in front of me. It was titled *Think and Grow Rich,* a popular title on human development by one of my favourite authors at the time. I put the book down because it occurred to me it was the fourth book on personal growth and development I was reading that month. The others, like the one I had just put down, lay in a neat pile on the right corner of my black compressed-wood office desk.

Only two months prior, I had gone on a shopping spree for books on human development. I was consumed by a voracious appetite for any information that possessed the potential of explaining some aspect of the great mystery of life. What was so phenomenal about my particular curiosity? Nothing perhaps, but suffice it to say, I felt possessed by it. There seemed to be no way for me to preclude my thoughts from incessantly hovering above this sense of curiosity. My interest was prisoner to studies in psychology and philosophy, two subjects that at the time were eons away from my entrepreneurial endeavours. Four hundred dollars later, I had procured enough books to constitute a small but respectable library. My entire collection at that moment stood at ninety-seven titles. I was on a resolute journey to a successful conclusion.

In May, the previous month, I had sold my IBM computer for three hundred dollars, losing over twelve hundred dollars of its purchase price in eleven months. This sale enabled me to top up the seventeen hundred dollars I had in cash to pay for the Dr. Richard Bandler seminar on Neuro-Linguistic Programming taking place in downtown Toronto. Neuro-Linguistic Programming proclaimed itself as a "science" that taught participants to unleash their full mental potential through the knowledge of how linguistics significantly impacts neurology. As though my NLP enrolment was not enough, I was also enrolled in a three-hour presentation titled How to Reduce Clutter in Your Life, facilitated by a supposed expert on "Efficiency and Time Management."

There seemed to be an abundance of such courses in those days. There were many times I aspired to be like some of the presenters. You see, once you feel committed to a journey of discovery such as I felt at that point in my life, your curiosity propels you down many paths. You wander down these paths until you have learned enough to invoke the momentum to branch off in another direction you hope will harbour real clues to life's mysteries. At times the path that is chosen is not well traveled; sometimes, not at all. The latter, to my mind, is the fabric with which "discovery" is woven. It never ceases to thrill me that I could one day uncover a truth about existence that has not been exposed before. A brand new frontier! Enlightenment!

The seminar on "clutter reduction" was going to take place later on in the week at the Learning Annex, an innovative quasi-academic establishment for students like myself. The Learning Annex played host to a conflagration of "experts," most of who were published authors. These "experts" delivered talks on their works, or as was usually the case, encapsulated their works in a three-hour oration to time-starved devotees like myself.

I was twenty-three years old, operating a lingerie wholesale and retail venture that seemed frozen in time, and spending mountains of money on personal growth and development. No one could challenge me for not investing in myself. I had always wanted to know why life worked as it does. Why were some people successful at their endeavours while others merely managed to get by? I wanted to construe why some people succumbed, and why many derived merriment out of their inclinations to subject others to their personal wills and whims, rather than enabling those people to blossom by exercising their own wills. I wanted to know why racism existed in society, not as a psychological explanation, but rather as a philosophical, even spiritual, cause. Why had human beings reduced themselves to categorization, to a form of human commoditization? I wanted to know why so many people despised others when, in fact, we have so much in common that could enable us to strive towards what would benefit all of us.

One of my deepest yearnings had always been to discover why god created a world in which there is so much injustice, so much pain, suffering, and often times, an overwhelming sense of destitution. And yet, in the same breath, there is so much wonderment, beauty, and serenity, an abundance of food, vegetation, oceans, rain forests, animals, the solar system, the ecosystem, and the spectacular genius of humanity.

I was baffled as to why such an abundance of food was so unevenly distributed to the extent that so many of god's "children" in various parts of the world, through no fault of their own, starved to death each and every passing day. This scandalous situation continues to manifest, while in North America alone, restaurants throw food out on a daily basis, enough to feed thousands of starving people.

Why was it the Israelis and Palestinians continued to engage in bitter fighting for such a prolonged period over a matter as simple as a piece of land that can be easily shared? Why were there attempts at genocide in Rwanda and many other parts of the world? What sort of person or spirit, professedly good, would commission, expressly or by implication, transgressions like the slavery of the African race; Napoleon Bonaparte's thirst for conquest at any cost; Adolf Hitler's massacres in Europe? Did god banish us to this pitiful state? To top it off, some of the religions of the world, humanity's attempt to reach its origins, then declare we are guilty of original sin! Who would construct a man, render him blind, endow him with a chronic liver ailment, cause him to lose both his parents in a car accident when he is seven years old, and then culminate such creation by ensuring that at the wonderful age of twenty-five, he encounters a serious car accident that leaves him with no legs?

Such was my state of mind as I sat glued to my swivel chair with my fingers matted in front of me. My elbows rested squarely on the slim leather arms of the chair while I pondered the avalanche of questions that had come to constitute the majority of my endeavours. Why was the state of humankind as it were? Was it all happenstance? Could it be that it was just a brilliant accident? But how could such order and symmetry, the structure upon which the cosmos and human physiology meticulously operate, exist by virtue of some inexplicable cosmic accident? My reason repelled the thought and could not accept it. There had to be a cause for all of it; a beginning. A beginning grand enough to befit the status humanity has seized for itself and seemingly orchestrated with deliberation and purpose. All my life I had been told that such a beginning was a nice old gentleman residing in the tranquility of the heavens where he rained havoc and love all at once on his creations. On this day, to my mind, this old man resembled an egotistical, self-serving, sadist, evil manipulator, and not what I expected "god" to be.

"If that is what you are, you might as well strike me dead right this minute, because this puppet is not about to participate in this unholy game of yours!"

I said this out aloud without contemplation and surprised myself. To this day, I do not recall another day when I had been quite as angry as I became at that moment. I remember rising somewhat unsteadily to my feet, expecting a catastrophe to arrest me, such as the walls of my office caving in. There was however, only silence. It was thick and murky, and caused me to perspire profusely. Sandra, the lady who helped me with my company's books, had retired for the day, and it seemed that most of the other third floor occupants had followed her lead.

My chest muscles seemed to tighten. Was I in the preliminary stages of a heart attack? I waited. The silence had grown so heavy by now, I was beginning to experience some difficulty breathing. I, Sam Tita, a mere mortal, was challenging the "most high" god! I quietly expected to begin disintegrating as castigation for my impertinence. I looked around the office nervously, only to discover I was still alone, and intact. I waited a while longer for the wrath of god to befall me, but nothing happened. Slowly, I regained some of my vehemence, even though this time, it was mildly diluted by a twinge of fear.

"Who the hell do you think you are?" I queried. "Some brand of coward for sure. You cannot even show your face!"

I waited some more, by now, completely oblivious of the passage of time. After what seemed like five or ten minutes, a wave of sensibility touched me on the shoulder, and being the objective, sensible person I considered myself to be, I heeded. Was I missing something? Was it possible that someone capable of creating such virtues as compassion, love, friendship, happiness and the incessant hunger for knowledge could harbour such arrogance? It seemed terribly paradoxical, to say the least.

"I'll make a pact with you right here, right now," I said, with my eyes cast to the ceiling.

"Show yourself to me, and I promise you, I'll give up everything and every dream I have and make sure the world knows who you are. And even after that, I will not stop. I will keep on going till the day I die."

I was trembling gently. A cold sweat made its way down my forehead and onto the bridge of my nose. I wiped it off and waited.

"Please, please, show yourself to me."

My anger was melting and in its place a sense of futility was creeping in. I waited, and waited. Nothing happened. I lowered my head, shaking it from side to side, at the conclusion of how useless it all was—my request, my anger, my curiosity. There were, after all, no empirical accounts of god having exposed himself to righteous people like Mahatma Gandhi, Mother Teresa, the Dalai Lama, Martin Luther King Jr., or any of the numerous people of spiritual prominence in our world. Why would god make himself known to me?

Deciding it was time to retire to my family and feeling quite exhausted mentally, I made my way to the washroom down the hall. It was going to be a long drive home and just in case I ran into dense traffic on the highway, I did not wish to compound my frustration with having to manage a full bladder. After completing my conference with nature, I went over to the sink, leaned ever so slightly to avoid getting my shirt soaked, and began washing my hands. It was while I was engaged in this most simple of activities that a door that had hung ajar throughout history, and yet had remained mysteriously invisible, suddenly burst open.

I was staring at the face of god in the mirror! My life would never be the same again.

•••••

That erroneous conclusion that I arrived at on that life-changing day in June 1992 propelled me down a path of convoluted philosophies that concluded with the formation of the foundation of a Theo-philosophy I would call "Deitology," which would propose that the sum total of the thinking of humankind would constitute the most efficient concept of god the world would have ever known. The trick was to find a way to unify the thinking of the world, which is obviously an impossible task. It is hard enough getting a husband wife to think alike even after several decades of marriage, much less getting the entire world to agree on any one thing.

LESSONS FROM RECONSTRUCTING GOD

Since becoming a believer in Jesus I have had time to reflect on the material I put in *Reconstructing God*. My reason for doing this has been to discover any truths and lies that I could articulate to help prevent someone else from going down the same very slippery slope that could easily have been the greatest mistake I ever made. The following five points capture the spirit of those reflections.

1. God is the one in control. He will not dance to your music.
2. Be humble in your search for God. Your arrogance will not move Him.
3. Seek God just for who He is. Discard every other agenda, such as wanting to prove something to the world.
4. The company you keep and the books you read will influence the direction of your thinking.

5. There is only one ultimate truth. It is Jesus, who is "the way, the truth and the life."

You don't have to waste many years of your life like I did, investigating every philosophy in the world, before coming to the realization that you actually just wasted your precious time. One of my biggest regrets has always been over the fact that I missed out on the experience of God's overflowing Grace in my life for many, many years as I pursued everything else in the world but Him.

My consolation, on the other hand, is that God's Grace is like a sweet melody that has neither a beginning nor an end. It doesn't matter when you start hearing it, because you can never miss any of its sweetness. Therefore when I deliberately entered into the experience of the abundance of God's goodness and mercy by inviting Him into my life to be my personal Lord and Saviour, it was as though I'd never really been away from it at any time. It is truly a supernatural experience.

You too can begin experiencing that overflowing Grace today. It is a gift that no one can pay for or earn in some way or other. Even if your understanding of its nuances feels less than complete, you can still begin enjoying its blessings.

You need to do three things:

1. Reflect on the things you've done wrong in your life.
2. If you feel sorry about them, tell God so.
3. Then say this simple prayer:

Dear God, I'm sorry for all the things I have done wrong in my life. I'm sorry for hurting the people I hurt, for doing things I shouldn't have done and for not doing the things I should have done. I'm asking You today to come into my life and take control. I'm asking You today to become my Lord and Saviour, and to lead and guide me for the rest of my life. I say this prayer in the name of

Your son Jesus Christ, who died on the cross for my sins. Amen.

Today you've become a child of God. His Grace will no longer be unpredictable events in your life but will surround you, protect you, lead you, provide for you and challenge you to enter into your destiny with boldness of mind and spirit. God's solemn promise to you from this day onward is never to leave you or abandon you, just as Moses said to Joshua when he passed on the mantle of his ministry to him: *"And the LORD, He is the One who goes before you. He will be with you; He will not leave you nor forsake you; do not fear nor be dismayed"* (Deuteronomy 31:8, NKJV).

The March of Destiny

6

If you said the short prayer in the previous chapter and invited Jesus Christ into your life to be your Lord and Saviour, then you are saved. This means that your spirit is renewed and forever cleaved to the Spirit of God. If you happen to have been close to God in the past but for one reason or the other you fell out of love with Him, yet you said the prayer again, you have renewed your vows to God and pledged your life to Him all over again. Congratulations, because like I mentioned earlier in this discourse, you will *never* arrive at your God-ordained destiny until you surrender your mind, heart and spirit to Him.

You may not realize it, but your salvation is by far the greatest demonstration of God's Grace in your life. Now you know beyond the shadow of a doubt where you will spend eternity, because now you are a bona fide child of the Creator of the world. This is what Jesus says in John:

> *Let not your heart be troubled; you believe in God, believe also in Me. In My Father's house are many mansions; if it were not so, I would have told you. I go to prepare a place for you. And if I go and prepare a place for you, I will come again and receive you to Myself; that where I am, there you may be also. And where I go you know, and the way you know.* (14:1-4, **NKJV**)

Your decision to know God gives you the assurance of eternity in heaven with Him, where the serenity and opulence are too fantastic to fathom. This is not just conjecture on my part, because the Bible tells us that the streets of heaven are paved with gold. *"The twelve gates were twelve pearls: each individual gate was of one pearl. And the street of the city was pure gold, like transparent glass"* (Revelation 21:21, NKJV).

But how do you describe the luxuriousness of the interior of a Rolls Royce if you've never ridden in one? How do you describe the opulence of the fabled Burj Al Arab hotel in Dubai, with its $20,000 a night royal suite, without actually experiencing it firsthand? The description of heaven is too much for the human mind to perceive even in imagination. Yet that is the promise of God to those who believe in Him. That is now your entitlement also. What a truly magnificent promise and the hope of everyone who believes in Jesus!

But it doesn't end there. When God created humankind in the beginning, His intention was not for us to live ordinary and mediocre lives here on earth and to wait to get to heaven before experiencing His provision at such a supernatural level. Here once again is the account of God's original intention for humankind at the time of creation: *"Then God said, 'Let Us make man in Our image, according to Our likeness; let them have dominion over the fish of the sea, over the birds of the air, and over the cattle, over all the earth and over every creeping thing that creeps on the earth'"* (Genesis 1:26, NKJV).

Therefore when you become saved there's a spiritual shift in your destiny because now you are beginning again from the beginning, when dominion and greatness were embedded into the very fabric your destiny. But how do you interpret Genesis 1:26? Do you become an animal tamer? Are you supposed to walk up to lions and tigers and command them to bow before you? I don't believe you're a silly person, but just for the sake of clarity, the answer is "No!"

What Genesis 1:26 is saying to you is that when you re-enter the original state of your destiny you once again become a child of the King of all kings. That is a position that comes with authority and power. However, you have to exercise that power with wisdom and humility the way Jesus did while He walked the face of the earth. You are designed and destined for greatness. You are a natural born ruler even though you may not feel like it. You have the power to command things into being and speak into circumstances and see them change. However your power today comes from and is found only in Jesus, because after humankind lost everything because of Adam's sin, it was Jesus who bought it all back for us.

Your authority on earth is through Jesus Christ. The great advantage in this is that you don't have to learn how to be a king. You don't even have to learn how to rule. God has made it very easy for you and me, because as long as His Word says things should be in a particular way, all you have to do is speak and declare it *in the name of Jesus* and watch it happen. That is the power conferred to you by Genesis 1:26 under the New Covenant in Jesus Christ.

God went even further to simplify our role as rulers on earth, so that we can fully harness and exercise all the power and authority that He established through Jesus for us. He has issued two major edicts by which you and I should live as believers and by which you can harvest the destiny that He wrote into your DNA at the time of your creation. They are:

1. Seek God first.

Jesus says,

Do not worry about your life, what you will eat or what you will drink; nor about your body, what you will put on. Is not life more than food and the body more than clothing? Look at the birds of the air, for they neither sow nor reap nor gather into barns; yet your heavenly Father feeds them. Are you not of more value than they? Which of you by worrying can add one cubit to his stature? So why do you worry about clothing? Consider the lilies of the field, how

*they grow: they neither toil nor spin; and yet I say to you that even
Solomon in all his glory was not arrayed like one of these. Now if
God so clothes the grass of the field, which today is, and tomorrow
is thrown into the oven, will He not much more clothe you, O you
of little faith? Therefore do not worry, saying, 'What shall we
eat?' or 'What shall we drink?' or 'What shall we wear?' For
after all these things the Gentiles seek. For your heavenly Father
knows that you need all these things. But seek first the kingdom of
God and His righteousness, and all these things shall be added to
you. Therefore do not worry about tomorrow, for tomorrow will
worry about its own things. Sufficient for the day is its own
trouble.* (Matthew 6:25-34, NKJV)

In the this passage Jesus addresses the most basic of human
necessities such as food, shelter and clothing. God is saying that He
is personally concerned about everything that concerns our lives.
Therefore we should quit worrying about the things we need in life
and to instead go after the things that He has purposed in our lives,
and in the process all our necessities will be met.

God is not suggesting that you shouldn't work for a living or
that you should enrol in a seminary tomorrow and become a pastor
or a missionary or an apostle. What God is saying is that when you
get up in the morning to go to work, you should be doing so in the
knowledge that working is merely a means to earn a living and is
not your life. God is saying that you should always be working on
a project for Him, to propagate the agenda of His Kingdom. While
you study for your nursing degree, you should be serving God at
your church at the same time. Then you should be praying for a
great job with a great pay package, so that you can invest greatly
into the work of God at your church and through other trusted
ministries. God is saying that your reason for getting up from sleep
and going about your day and even pursuing a career should be
ultimately to promote His agenda in the world. God promises that

as long as we keep Him at the forefront of our lives and go after the things that He needs to get done on earth with diligence and passion, then He will ensure that we never lack for anything. That is our basic assurance.

2. TAKE CARE OF GOD'S BUSINESS FIRST.

Seeking God should be the primary endeavour of every human being. However, seeking God is only one part of a two-part subject, because we can seek God and all the things that He stands for yet come short of *doing* the things He has asked us to do as a demonstration of our love, appreciation and obedience.

God is a reasonable and rational God. To that extent He knows that we are busy people; He did create us, after all. He has therefore made it *really* easy for us to demonstrate our love and willingness to serve Him. He has spelled it out for us so that in our *busyness* we don't have to try to figure it out but can just go ahead and do it. Just thinking about it is not sufficient. You have to go ahead and actually do what God wants to be done.

God's Business in the Physical Realm

Jesus couldn't be clearer about what is important to Him, as demonstrated by the following passage:

When the Son of Man comes in His glory, and all the holy angels with Him, then He will sit on the throne of His glory. All the nations will be gathered before Him, and He will separate them one from another, as a shepherd divides his sheep from the goats. And He will set the sheep on His right hand, but the goats on the left. Then the King will say to those on His right hand, "Come, you blessed of My Father, inherit the kingdom prepared for you from the foundation of the world: for I was hungry and you gave Me food; I was thirsty and you gave Me drink; I was a stranger and you took Me in; I was naked and you clothed Me;

I was sick and you visited Me; I was in prison and you came to Me." Then the righteous will answer Him, saying, "Lord, when did we see You hungry and feed You, or thirsty and give You drink? When did we see You a stranger and take You in, or naked and clothe You? Or when did we see You sick, or in prison, and come to You?" And the King will answer and say to them, "Assuredly, I say to you, inasmuch as you did it to one of the least of these My brethren, you did it to Me." (Matthew 25:31-40, NKJV)

He wants us to each

- Feed the poor
- Give shelter to those in need
- Clothe those who have none
- Visit (and pray) for the sick
- Visit (and minister) to those in jail

It is my duty, and yours, to feed, clothe, comfort and pray for those in need, in the name of Jesus.

Why must it be in the name of Jesus?

God will not shun good works not done in the name of His Son Jesus; however those good works in themselves will not get anyone the salvation that gives eternal life. The reason is that God desires your trust much more than He desires your obedience. That is why He did not ask you and me to obey Jesus as the pre-requisite for salvation, but rather God asked you and me to trust in Jesus so that we can be saved. When you cater to the needy and the weary in the name of Jesus, you are in fact demonstrating your trust in Him.

A Double Trust Requirement

Recognize that there is a double trust requirement involved here, which should hammer home the fact of the importance of helping the needy in the name of Jesus:

- Remember first that God could have designed us to be obedient, but He didn't and instead gave us the ability to choose or reject Him freely.
- Remember secondly that God could have demanded that we obey His Son Jesus Christ or perish in hell for all eternity, but He didn't.
- Rather, He asked us to believe in Him, which is the same as trusting Him, and then we will be saved.

Here is the double trust requirement; you have to trust God's Word (the Bible) enough to believe what it says when it tells you that trusting Jesus is the only way to be saved. Then you have to go ahead and trust in Jesus in order to receive your salvation.

Trust is crucial in life, and the kingdom of God is no different. This is why the one who does good works and helps people outside of the name of Jesus is applauded but is not guaranteed salvation. Your obedience means nothing to God if you don't first of all trust Him. Even though He still smiles at you for helping out, when Jesus is kept out of the equation God knows you're just really telling Him that you don't trust Him fully.

You probably observed in Matthew 25:31-40 that Jesus is addressing the physical needs of a desperate world. They are the basic needs that a person must enjoy in order to stay alive. He or she who supplies those needs gains the attention of the one attended to. What a fertile ground to plant the truth of the world, which is the Word of God, right after supplying a critical physical need that a desperate soul needs, such as a warm meal or a warm blanket.

SAM TITA

God's Business in the Spiritual Realm

To attend to the spiritual needs of our desperate world, Jesus issued the ultimate directive just as He was about to return to heaven, only a short while after His brutal crucifixion, death and resurrection. This is what He commanded those of us who are called His disciples to do:

> *All authority has been given to Me in heaven and on earth.* **Go therefore and make disciples of all the nations**, *baptizing them in the name of the Father and of the Son and of the Holy Spirit, teaching them to observe all things that I have commanded you; and lo, I am with you always, even to the end of the age.* (Matthew 28:18-20, NKJV, emphasis added)

This passage is what is reverently known as *the great commission* and is the duty of everyone who is called a follower of Jesus Christ. God has ordained you and me as evangelists who are to go into our places of work, the grocery store, the coffee house and across oceans and continents to tell the world about Jesus. When we do this we come full circle. We cater to the physical needs of those who are in want and then tell them the redeeming message of the gospel of Jesus, who is the Messiah of the world.

If the purpose of God for your life is the only way you can enter into and walk in your destiny, without which you're no better than a leaf in the wind, then it makes absolute sense that you enter into your destiny today and begin the march that will bring you the joy that trumps all your troubles and the fulfillment that destroys boredom.

Jesus has issued the marching order for all who believe in Him. The question now is, how do you go about it? How do you begin? Where do you start? This is the question that paralyzes many believers who have a heart to serve God but for one reason or the other have not done so yet.

When I hosted the Crossroads Television live ministry broadcast called *Nite Lite Live*, I very often encountered callers who were convinced in their hearts that God has called them to ministry (and He has) but who found themselves frozen by either fear or a lack of understanding caused by the often terrifying question "How?"

We'll address the question in the paragraphs and chapters that follow. If you embrace the simple teaching that will follow, your identity will automatically change, and you will become a weapon of mass destruction in the camp of liars, where the enemy of the Truth abides. Or, if you have a gentle spirit like my wife, then instead of considering yourself a weapon of mass destruction, you may want to see yourself as a bearer of the testimony of Jesus, like my worship pastor, Joel Chambers, of Global Kingdom Ministries put it. Either way, please follow me.

REVIEW SUMMARY

- Your mind has opened up to allow Jesus into your life, and now you are saved.
- You love God for forgiving your sins.
- You appreciate all that He's done in your life, even way back before you were saved.
- You trust Him enough to allow Him to take control of your life.
- You understand that life apart from Jesus is a waste of time.
- You understand that your life only means something when you live for God and His purpose.
- You realize that you will never enter your true destiny without executing God's purpose for your life.
- You love God enough to want to execute that purpose no matter what.

Now you want to know how to join and enter into the march of your destiny.

THE HIERARCHY OF
DESTINY

7

Before I continue to expound on the marching orders of every Christian, found in Matthew 28:18-20, I want to bring your attention to a subtle but important distinction in our relationship with Jesus that is rarely articulated. At the end of this brief exposition you will have to answer a question, and the answer you provide will define your willingness, commitment and effectiveness in carrying out the assignment given to you by Jesus Christ Himself.

In John is nestled a curious verbal exchange between Jesus and Peter that many people are familiar with but just as many people simply overlook:

> *So when they had eaten breakfast, Jesus said to Simon Peter, "Simon, son of Jonah, do you love Me more than these?"*
> *He said to Him, "Yes, Lord; You know that I love You."*
> *He said to him, "Feed My lambs."*
> *He said to him again a second time, "Simon, son of Jonah, do you love Me?"*
> *He said to Him, "Yes, Lord; You know that I love You."*
> *He said to him, "Tend My sheep."*
> *He said to him the third time, "Simon, son of Jonah, do you love*

Me?" Peter was grieved because He said to him the third time,
"Do you love Me?"
And he said to Him, "Lord, You know all things; You know that
I love You."
Jesus said to him, "Feed My sheep. Most assuredly, I say to you,
when you were younger, you girded yourself and walked where you
wished; but when you are old, you will stretch out your hands,
and another will gird you and carry you where you do not wish."
This He spoke, signifying by what death he would glorify God.
And when He had spoken this, He said to him, "Follow Me."
(21:15-19, NKJV)

Jesus asked Peter if he loved Him three times, and Peter
responded "yes" three times. Then each time Peter responded, Jesus
gave Peter a command to:

- Feed His lambs
- Tend His sheep
- Feed His sheep

And then finally Jesus asked Peter to follow Him.

Many Christians read through the quoted passage and merely
attribute the exchange between Jesus and Peter to the fact that
Peter had denied Jesus three times just days before, and Jesus was
looking for reassurance from Peter. That was not the case at all.

I mentioned previously that the disciples had lost all hope
when Jesus hung on the cross and breathed what they thought was
His last breath, because they had not understood what He meant
when He said He would be raised from the dead on the third day.
Afraid for his life, Peter had denied being associated with Jesus, but
there is no mention anywhere in the Bible that Peter had stopped
believing in Jesus for even a moment.

Therefore when Jesus repeatedly asked Peter if he loved Him,
it wasn't because Jesus did not know that Peter believed in Him.

On the contrary, Jesus knew quite well that Peter believed in Him. In fact, Jesus also knew that Peter loved Him. However Jesus was after something else. He needed Peter to also know for himself that he (Peter) indeed loved Him, because of the weight of the assignment he was about to receive from Jesus.

Jesus knows that believing in Him is important. But He also knows that because you believe in Him Satan will target you for destruction. In the days of trials and stresses, it is the love for Jesus that enables a believer to stare Satan right in the face and say, "Buzz off!" It is the love for Jesus that will enable believers to fight the temptations thrown at them to cause them to sin. Jesus was after Peter's heart, and not just His mind. Essentially Jesus was equating loving Him with doing His will; He was saying to Peter that if Peter loved Him he would take care of His flock, which are His children, that being you and me.

We gather the following from that exchange:

1. You can believe in Jesus but not love Him (otherwise He wouldn't be asking Peter).
2. If you love Jesus you will feed and tend His sheep (because that is His desire).

Jesus went on to entrust Peter with the responsibility of organizing and heading the Church in all the earth, which Peter did excellently together with the other disciples even to his death when Emperor Nero of Rome killed him in AD 64 for refusing to recant statements that Jesus had in fact risen from the dead like He said He would. What an incredible responsibility!

Jesus is God, and like Peter said, *"Lord, You know all things; You know that I love You."* Jesus knows those who just believe in Him so that they will not perish in hell and those who have gone beyond just believing in Him and also love Him. I believe Jesus wanted us to know categorically that anyone who is not heeding to the call of the evangelist on earth, to feed and tend to His flock, cannot truly love Him. It doesn't mean that they don't believe in Him; it doesn't mean that they are not saved. However, they don't love Him enough to desire to take care of what belongs to Him.

Here is the distinction in the hierarchy of destiny therefore: there are Jesus believers and Jesus lovers in the kingdom of God.

JESUS BELIEVERS

- Are saved
- Want all the blessings of God
- But don't want to give anything back to God
- Whine about not having time to serve God
- Frown when they pay their tithes or don't tithe at all

JESUS LOVERS

- Believe in Jesus
- Are saved
- Want all the blessings of God
- Do things to serve and please God
- Don't whine about making time to serve God
- Are glad to pay their tithes (even when it hurts)

Are you a Jesus believer or a Jesus lover? Remember the last time you were deeply in love with someone? Do you remember how badly you wanted to do things that would make him or her happy? When people fall out of love with each other, for the most part it is because they cease seeing each other as special to each other. They cease doing things to surprise and please each other. Very often this state of lack of excitement in a relationship is not the product of something having gone wrong in the relationship, but rather it is the very cause of everything going wrong in the relationship.

The surest way to fall out of love with the Saviour of your soul and the author of your destiny is to not serve Him. By asking Peter three times whether he loved Him, Jesus is asking you if you just believe in Him so that you will not perish, or if indeed you love Him the way you sing about in church on Sunday. Because if indeed you do truly love Him, just like He commanded Peter you too must feed His sheep and tend His flock. Once again, are you a Jesus believer or a Jesus lover?

Your answer determines your placement in the hierarchy of destiny. This may come as a big surprise to many Christians, but the Bible makes it clear that all Christians are not rewarded equally by God:

> *Then Jesus said to His disciples, "If anyone desires to come after Me, let him deny himself, and take up his cross, and follow Me. For whoever desires to save his life will lose it, but whoever loses his life for My sake will find it. For what profit is it to a man if he gains the whole world, and loses his own soul? Or what will a man give in exchange for his soul? For the Son of Man will come in the glory of His Father with His angels, and then He will reward each according to his works."* (Matthew 16:24-27, NKJV)

God wants your help to propagate the message of His redemptive Grace to the ends of the world so that the souls of many can be saved. Let's go on now to explore the simplest and most effective way to demonstrate your love for Jesus.

DECLARING YOUR LOVE FOR JESUS—WITH WORDS

Love is a *doing* word; it is an active word. Love is not just what your lips declare but also what your actions demonstrate. As a matter of fact, there is more of the substance of love in your actions than in your verbal declarations, because to most people talk is cheap. Anyone can say anything but not mean it just because the words are free. They are powerful, but they cost nothing.

What good is it for a husband to tell his wife he loves her at night when he desires to make love to her, just to slam the door in her face in the morning because she is a little late getting to the car to go to work? Doing such a thing erases the meaning of his sweet words from the night before. Those sweet words are terrific; don't get me wrong. However they must necessarily be followed by corroborating actions. That's the combination that seals up happy marriages that last a lifetime.

Jesus delights in a relationship with you in which there is a regular exchange of sweet words. Numerous times He tells us just how much He loves us in the Bible, and there are also many wonderful promises He has spoken to those who accept Him as their Saviour. But He also wants action, just like He demonstrated when He allowed Himself to be brutalized to death in order to redeem us from the burden of our sins.

On your part you should make it a point to tell Jesus sweet things. When you speak with Him it mustn't always be about asking Him for something. I know He doesn't mind that you ask Him for things. In fact He wants you to ask Him for things. However, you should speak to Him sometimes and just tell Him how much you love and appreciate Him. Thank Him for what He's done in your life.

Use words like King David used on one of the many occasions when he reminded God of God's goodness to him. I have personalized it so that you can speak it to Jesus on your own behalf. The reference is Psalm 18:1-19.

I will love You, O LORD, my strength.
You are my rock and my fortress and my deliverer;
My God, my strength, in whom I will trust;
My shield and the horn of my salvation, my stronghold.
I will call upon You, who is worthy to be praised;
So shall I be saved from my enemies.

When the pangs of death surrounded me
And the floods of ungodliness made me afraid;

Deciding to Know God in a Deeper Way

When the sorrows of hell surrounded me
and the snares of death confronted me;
In my distress I called upon You,
And cried out to You, my God;
You heard my voice from Your temple,
And my cry came before You, even to Your ears.

Then the earth shook and trembled
The foundations of the hills also quaked and were shaken,
because You were angry.
Smoke went up from Your nostrils,
And devouring fire from Your mouth;
Coals were kindled by it.

You bowed the heavens also, and came down
With darkness under Your feet.
And You rode upon a cherub, and flew;
You flew upon the wings of the wind.
You made darkness Your secret place;
Your canopy around You was dark waters
And thick clouds of the skies.
From the brightness before You
Your thick clouds passed with hailstones and coals of fire.

You, my LORD, thundered from heaven,
And You, the Most High, uttered Your voice,
Hailstones and coals of fire.
You sent out Your arrows and scattered the foe,
Lightnings in abundance, and You vanquished them.
Then the channels of the sea were seen,
The foundations of the world were uncovered
At Your rebuke, O LORD,
At the blast of the breath of Your nostrils.

You sent from above, You took me;
You drew me out of many waters.
You delivered me from my strong enemy,
From those who hated me,
For they were too strong for me.
They confronted me in the day of my calamity,
But You, my LORD, were my support.
You also brought me out into a broad place;
You delivered me because You delighted in me.

When I reflect on these sweet words of praise to God, I imagine an eighteen-year-old boy having a conversation with his father in which he reminisces about a time when he was perhaps six years old and the neighbourhood bully was chasing him down the street. But then suddenly, unexpected and seemingly out of nowhere, his father showed up. He thundered at the bully angrily and chased him away, sparing his son the injury that the bully was sure to inflict on him. In such a time of reminiscing the son is not asking the father for anything. He is simply bringing to his father's remembrance one of many times when his father saved him from certain pain. I can see his father smiling from ear to ear as he listens, remembering the delight it's been to raise his boy. In such a time of sweet fellowship the bond of father and son grows stronger and a milestone is planted in the timeline of their relationship.

There is great power in such a moment, and Jesus longs for such fellowship with you, His child. Don't be constrained by the words in the passage above either, because you alone know the pits from which God has pulled you to save you from pain and danger. Therefore bring it to His remembrance in praise, and worship Him for being God in your life. Do it often, like David did.

It was this attribute of awe for His God that spared David's soul in spite of his terrible wrongs, which included murder and adultery. He was human and faltered often. But as soon as he came to his senses, he cried out to God, begging Him for forgiveness and giving Him praise. And then even when he hadn't done anything wrong, he would praise God like no one else could in all of Israel. That pleased God very much.

DECLARING YOUR LOVE FOR JESUS—WITH ACTION

Action is the realization of your thinking. It is the corroboration of your verbal declarations. It is the testimony of your commitment and your imprint on the manuscript of your life. Without action nothing happens, and the world becomes a Cameroonian fish market with no fish to sell. It is utter chaos and a massive waste of time.

Imagine for a moment that when Jesus came to the earth all He did was talk about the Kingdom of God, without demonstrating the power of that Kingdom through signs and wonders such as instantaneous healing of the sick and raising the dead to life. Imagine just for a moment that after He allowed Himself to be brutalized to death and hung on the cross like a common thief, He failed to rise up from the tomb and make Himself visible to a multitude of eyewitnesses, who ultimately succumbed to torture and death because of their testimonies. Imagine that all He ever did was talk, talk, talk. Only a fool would have believed Him then.

Imagine that even today there were no signs and wonders; what if there was just talking and preaching and nothing else? What if no one ever got healed from their diseases or experienced the supernatural hand of God in their finances and relationships? How would people believe in God then? The world would be right to label a person like me as being delusional, because I would be talking about indemonstrable things. But thank God that I have a testimony! As a matter of fact, I thank God that I have numerous testimonies of His healing power in my life and in my family. I thank Him that His amazing Grace saved our home from being auctioned off even when I made a large mistake in judgment. I thank Him for supernaturally restoring my marriage even after I bungled it up so badly for so many years.

For these and other reasons I believe in Him with all my heart, with all of my thinking and with my resources. I put my money where my mouth is. That in itself is a manifestation of His Grace in my life.

Action therefore is crucial in life, because like I have mentioned elsewhere, words are free and talk is cheap. You could have dreamed of having the job you have for ten years, but until you got off the couch and actually did something about it, it wouldn't have materialized. You can tell your children how much you're going to provide for then—a nice home, good cars, good food and entertainment and all the good things in life—but until you actually provide these things for them, you haven't. It's really that simple. This is not suggesting that life cannot change the course of your plans, because it often will. But like Emmanuel Kant, the great 18th century German philosopher, said, it is your intention (and your action) that counts, and not the end result, because no one has control of ultimate outcomes except God.

Therefore attending church is both great and necessary. Studying the Word of God, which is encapsulated in the Bible, is imperative. Telling Jesus you love Him is wonderful. Praising and worshipping Him go without saying. However when it is all said and done, if you refuse to go out into the world to feed and clothe the hungry and to tell the world about Jesus, you have failed the one you claim to love so desperately. The chief reason Jesus came to this earth to die on the cross was so that by His death the souls of human beings all over the world would be gathered up and brought to God the Father. That is the chief reason *you* got saved. And now that you are, Jesus is asking you to tell others about it so that they too might be saved.

You probably noticed that when I described *action* earlier, it included both *telling* and *doing*. The reason is that your *doing* corroborates your *telling*. With that understanding then, here are some things you can do in order to reach the world for Jesus *with your actions*.

Attend Bible school (not a prerequisite, but it will help) and become:

- A Christian apologist
- An evangelist
- A pastor
- A prophet
- A Christian radio or television talk show host
- A Christian book or magazine writer
- A Christian music composer/writer/singer
- A Christian counsellor
- A Christian educator/teacher/professor
- A Christian movie-maker/producer/director

The list goes on and on.

I am one hundred percent in favour of all of the above because we Christians have become the minority in the world in the demonstration of influence and the propagation of our beliefs. That situation needs to change, and it will happen as Christians all over the world learn to make their influence felt in every facet of life.

Recently when I hosted *Nite Lite Live,* I made an appeal to the viewers to rise up and fight a new grade-school "sex education" curriculum in the Canadian province of Ontario that would involve grades one to nine students; the grade one students would be taught about their genitals and the differences thereof, while the higher grades would be taught the pleasures of masturbation, oral sex, homosexual intercourse, vaginal lubrication and anal sex! My appeal was not just for the viewers to rise up and fight the bill that proposed that atrocity but also to become militant and to pursue careers in every sector of the economy so that together we would promote Christian moral values as delineated by God in the Bible.

All of the above is to make the point that I am one hundred percent in favour of Christians pursuing careers that will enable them to do great things for the Kingdom of God, and to heed the call of the evangelist described in Matthew 28:18-20, which admonishes all of us to *"Go therefore and make disciples of all the nations"* (NKJV).

Note however that Jesus issued this command over two thousand years ago, and yet statistics indicate that only two out of every one hundred Christians of the twenty-first century will ever lead anyone to Christ. That means that wherever there is a gathering of fifty Christians, sadly, only one will ever lead anyone to Christ. It's no wonder then that Christians have become the minority in the exercising of influence in the world, and most Christians fail to experience the victory that we are entitled to through Jesus Christ.

THE SIMPLEST AND MOST EFFECTIVE TOOL OF MINISTRY

8

While you can aspire to, and indeed become very effective in any one of the domains listed previously and be positioned to influence the world for Jesus, by far the most important and most effective tool of ministry in the world is simply to *tell the world the truth about the Truth of the world.* That is in fact our ministry catchphrase. The word for it is to *testify.*

There is no other approach to spreading the gospel of Jesus Christ that is as effective as this one. By testifying you are telling the world what God has done in your life and why you love Him and worship Him and trust Him. In so doing you bring glory to the name of Almighty God and turn the eyes of the world towards Him.

There are many who don't quite understand what it means to testify or how to do it effectively. There are those who know what it means to testify and also know how to do it effectively, but then fail to testify. And then there are those who are eagerly testifying of God's goodness to them but are going about it the wrong way and are causing themselves embarrassment and making a mockery of God's precious name. I will cover all of these scenarios for two very important reasons:

1. So that your testimony can become a real destroyer of happiness for Satan, and
2. So that your testimony will become an act of deep and personal worship of our Father in heaven.

Let's start by defining what it means to testify.

This is the definition provided by the *Oxford English Dictionary*: To serve as evidence or proof that something exists or is the case. *Webster's Revised Unabridged Dictionary* offers this definition:

1. To make a solemn declaration, verbal or written, to establish some fact; to give testimony for the purpose of communicating to others a knowledge of something not known to them.
2. To bear witness to; to support the truth of by testimony; to affirm or declare solemnly.

You can say that to *testify*, therefore, is to declare the truth about your belief in Jesus by making statements based on your personal knowledge of Him, to serve as evidence of His Grace in your life. Your testimony is the evidence of the presence of and the manifestation of God's unmerited and supernatural love for you and through you. There is no more anointing in ministry than when you minister out of the abundance of your very own testimony. The apostle Paul wrote the following in his letter to the church in Rome:

> *Therefore I have reason to glory in Christ Jesus in the things which pertain to God. For I will not dare to speak of any of those things which Christ has not accomplished through me, in word and deed, to make the Gentiles obedient—in mighty signs and wonders, by the power of the Spirit of God, so that from Jerusalem and round about to Illyricum I have fully preached the gospel of Christ. And so I have made it my aim to*

preach the gospel, not where Christ was named, lest I should build on another man's foundation, but as it is written: "To whom He was not announced, they shall see; And those who have not heard shall understand." (Romans 15:17-21, NKJV, emphasis added)

In that passage the apostle Paul is telling the church in Rome that even though he had learned much, had seen much and had travelled much, he would only dare speak boldly about the things that Jesus had done in him and through him to bring the non-Jews to know God. Your testimony is the most powerful tool in your arsenal for all your ministry endeavours for the following reasons:

- It costs you nothing.
- You don't have to attend Bible school to obtain it.
- You don't have to be able to preach to use it.
- It is the most real experience of God you have.
- No one can challenge you successfully about it.
- You can speak about it with complete confidence.
- You can speak about it with total authority.
- All you need is one instance of God's Grace in your life to have a testimony.
- Your testimony is your seed for more testimonies.

I usually end this portion of my discourse on testifying with the fact that attending Bible school is a fantastic move that will inspire you and equip you and can make you significantly more effective in your witnessing for God. Unfortunately most Christians will never make it to Bible school, for numerous reasons. However, every Christian has a testimony.

Imagine what would happen in the world today if every Christian opened their mouth and testified to at least one non-Christian in their lifetime. Then imagine what would happen if every Christian testified to at least one non-Christian once a year, or perhaps once a month or once a week! We would turn the world "right-side up for Christ," as my pastor, the Reverend Bob Johnston, would say. The church of Jesus Christ on earth would once again experience the power and anointing that the early disciples knew, which enabled them to win thousands of souls at a time for Jesus, even with no microphones, television, Internet or even church buildings!

WHY TESTIFYING IS SO IMPORTANT

These are my top three reasons why your testimony is so very important:

1. When you testify you give God glory for what He has done in your life. In essence you tell the world that even though you look pretty and sound smart, and even though you seem like you have everything under control, if it wasn't for the Grace of God you would be nowhere.

The question that comes to mind is this: "What about all the people who are 'successful' in the world but have shut Jesus out of their lives?"

Your answer is that looks can be very deceiving. Many people only look successful, but when you zoom in on their lives you find things that would make you shake your head. Most of their lives are filled with things such as important careers, fancy cars and large houses that offer only a superficial level of satisfaction, and which oftentimes fail to do even that.

I remember being in a relationship with a woman I'd fallen in love with when my wife and I broke up. This lady was wealthy and very well known where we lived. Together we looked like the ideal couple—young, vivacious and successful. I drove an expensive car, and we lived in an exclusive part of town. But no one on the outside knew just how miserable we both were. She could not find complete satisfaction in the relationship, and I preferred to live on the roof of the house on most days. Yet we looked so good outwardly.

Then of course there is the fact that you have no idea what diseases some of these "successful" people are battling in their lives or the heartbreaks they're experiencing. Most often the grass only looks greener on the other side of the fence.

Take the case of Michael Jackson, who in my opinion was the ultimate pop star and epitomized Hollywood and all its glamour. I loved the man and his music. There was something gentle and fascinating about the way he did things. I grew up on his numerous chart-topping songs, and like many young people in my day, I had wanted to be just like him when I grew up. That was obviously a long time ago. Michael Jackson's face is still recognizable just about anywhere on earth, and his music continues to be extremely influential. Yet by his very words his life was miserable, to the extent that he had to have medications just to be able to fall asleep. As you may know, Michael died from medical complications during the administering of some of his medications by his personal doctor in 2009. His life looked glamorous from the outside, from where it seemed he had it all—fame and fortune. Yet from up close he was fundamentally a very unhappy person, in the context of true happiness as described in the Bible.

Hence your testimony tells the world that the peace you know, the healing you received, the job you have and your supernatural sense that all will be well are because God is in control of your life and His Grace rests with you. This attitude of gratitude glorifies the name of God and turns the world towards Him. Your testimony informs the world that all the money, fame and power in the world mean absolutely nothing if they don't revolve around God and His agenda for the world.

2.   Testifying has to do with you announcing to the world whose side you're on, God's or Satan's. This is very serious and defines the

level of audacity with which you live your life. In anything you do, you are most effective when you know your mission and are focused on it. A person who lives without focus is apt to vacillate frequently, shifting from one opinion to the next and from one idea to the next.

James wrote the following admonition to the people of Israel concerning those amongst them who had no focus in their faith:

If any of you lacks wisdom, let him ask of God, who gives to all liberally and without reproach, and it will be given to him. But let him ask in faith, with no doubting, for he who doubts is like a wave of the sea driven and tossed by the wind. For let not that man suppose that he will receive anything from the Lord; he is a double-minded man, unstable in all his ways. (James 1:5-8, NKJV)

Therefore when you testify to the world about the Grace of God in your life, you are saying to both the world and to yourself that you belong to God and you give Him credit for all He has done for you. But hold on, because here is the upshot: because you have opened your mouth once, twice, three times and more and have announced to the world what God has done for you, and in the process have let the world know that you belong to God, this very act serves as a guiding light in your life. The reason is that once the world has identified you as a child of God, they immediately raise their expectations of you in everything you do. They begin watching your every move and monitor how you deal with things. This puts you squarely where God wants you to be as described in His Word, where it states, "*You are the light of the world. A city that is set on a hill cannot be hidden. Nor do they light a lamp and put it under a basket, but on a lampstand, and it gives light to all who are in the house. Let your light so shine before men, that they may see your good works and glorify your Father in heaven*" (Matthew 5:14-16, NKJV).

If however you fail to testify, no one knows who you are or whose you are, and there are therefore no unique expectations of you, because you are deemed to be like everybody else, which you are not if you are a believer in Jesus Christ.

3. Testifying helps bring to your very own remembrance on a regular basis all the things God has done for you and for the ones you love and have prayed for. Your testimony is really the Word of God in action. Your testimony is the manifestation of the Word of God in your life, so that as often as you speak of it your faith grows, and you edify the spirits of the believers who hear you and glorify the name of God in the hearing of those who don't yet know Him. The apostle Paul wrote the following line to the Church in Rome: *"So then faith comes by hearing, and hearing by the word of God"* (Romans 10:17, NKJV).

Think about this: your testimony may be the only Word of God a person may ever hear before giving their life to Christ. And since faith comes by hearing the Word of God, when you testify your faith grows as you hear yourself testify. Your strong faith now places a bigger demand on God because He can trust you with more. Yes, trials will continue to come as they always do, but through it all you will live a more victorious life, which will be full of audacity because of what Jesus Christ has done for you and continues to do.

I have personally arrived at the place in my life where I testify at every opportunity about everything God has done for me, including my salvation. One of the points I pray about the most is that God should bring to my remembrance the many times He has walked me through the storms, fears and pains in my life, so that when I encounter another one of whatever breed or manifestation, I can rest assured that the same God who walked me through in the past is able to, has promised to, and will walk me through this time as well. Armed with this confidence I spend much less time whining and complaining about my problems. I do what I can on my part and literally abandon the rest to Jesus.

Very often it is at the point where our resources are stretched thin and our circumstances are close to the breaking point that God shows up to arrest the arresters of our peace and to bring calm back to our hearts. In such a place of desperation God's restorative Grace is both accentuated and better appreciated by its beneficiary.

Your testimony therefore is:

- A practical tool to help manage your everyday life stresses
- A spiritual muffler that blocks the voice of Satan from your ears
- An antidote if the voice of Satan manages to penetrate the walls of your thinking

As you may remember, in this section I am discussing my top three reasons why testifying is so important. To give you some more encouragement in this area, I want to show you the quality of the company you will be keeping if you make the decision today to become a testifier of the Truth to the world, based primarily and importantly on your personal experience with the Grace of God in its numerous manifestations. The following exposition is therefore intended to seal the discourse on the importance of testifying.

JESUS HIMSELF TESTIFIED

As we have seen before, to testify is to give a firsthand account of the truth about a situation based on personal knowledge and experience. Anything short of personal knowledge and experience is merely circumstantial and can be easily rebutted.

When I testify concerning God, I do so based on my personal experience of Him so that the world can get to know Him. I simply point the world to Him. That is really all you and I are expected to and can do.

However when Jesus testified concerning the things of God and of heaven, He did so to magnify the subjects and to shed light on them in a manner and depth that no one else could because no one else had the firsthand knowledge He did.

In John is one of many recorded instances when Jesus baffled the world with the depth and crispness of His testimony. In this instance He was en route to be crucified on the cross, and Pilate was looking for an opportunity to exonerate Him, if only He could say the "right" things, which to the Pharisees meant anything but the truth.

> *"You are a king, then!" said Pilate. Jesus answered, "You are right in saying I am a king. In fact, for this reason I was born, and for this I came into the world, to testify to the truth. Everyone on the side of truth listens to me."* (John 18:37, NIV)

THE APOSTLE PAUL ALSO TESTIFIED

The apostle Paul is credited for being used by God to write about one-third of the New Testament, so you know we're talking about a mighty man in the kingdom of God. The books he wrote are:

Romans

I Corinthians

II Corinthians

Galatians

Ephesians

Philippians

Colossians

I Thessalonians

II Thessalonians

1 Timothy

II Timothy
Philemon and
Hebrews

There is debate about whether or not Paul actually wrote
Hebrews because the original text is unsigned. My research leads me
to believe that he did but left the text unsigned by divine inspiration.
I mention this here so that you are not surprised if you encounter that
debate in the future as you pursue the knowledge of God.

The important point to make here is that Jesus, who is God,
testified, and so did Paul, whom Jesus personally called into ministry. As a matter of fact, Paul wrote in Romans 15:18 that in all
his teachings and preaching of the gospel of Jesus, he only dared to
talk about the things that Jesus used him to do personally. He did
not rely on his great philosophical knowledge, or even his knowledge of the Torah. Rather, he used all that he learned and knew
insofar as it accentuated his testimony concerning Jesus. Following
is one account of Paul's great zeal for testifying about Jesus:

> When Silas and Timothy had come from Macedonia, Paul was
> compelled by the Spirit, and testified to the Jews that Jesus is the
> Christ. But when they opposed him and blasphemed, he shook his
> garments and said to them, "Your blood be upon your own heads;
> I am clean. From now on I will go to the Gentiles." And he
> departed from there and entered the house of a certain man named
> Justus, one who worshiped God, whose house was next door to the
> synagogue. Then Crispus, the ruler of the synagogue, believed on
> the Lord with all his household. And many of the Corinthians,
> hearing, believed and were baptized.
>
> Now the Lord spoke to Paul in the night by a vision, "Do
> not be afraid, but speak, and do not keep silent; for I am with you,
> and no one will attack you to hurt you; for I have many people in
> this city." And he continued there a year and six months, teaching
> the word of God among them. (Acts 18:5-11, NKJV)

PETER, CHIEF STEWARD OF THE CHURCH ON EARTH, TESTIFIED

I'm referring to Peter, to whom Jesus gave the assignment of organizing His Church on earth. This is the same Peter who angrily cut off the ear of one of the officers who had come to arrest Jesus for crucifixion and who later on denied Jesus in order to avoid being killed. But Jesus knew Peter's love for Him, so He forgave Peter and restored him. Fresh with the memory of such incredible forgiveness and restoration, and coupled with the power of the Holy Spirit in him after Pentecost, Peter never looked back again. He travelled far and wide, giving his testimony of his personal encounter with the Saviour of the world. The following is recorded in Acts concerning Peter:

> And with many other words he testified and exhorted them, saying, "Be saved from this perverse generation." Then those who gladly received his word were baptized; and that day about three thousand souls were added to them. And they continued steadfastly in the apostles' doctrine and fellowship, in the breaking of bread, and in prayers. (Acts 2:40-42, NKJV)

What an amazing story. In just one day of testifying three thousand souls were brought into the kingdom of God! And all of this was done without the availability of radio, television or the Internet. There is neither any mention anywhere in the Bible where Peter is supposed to have attended Bible school. All he had was his personal encounter with Jesus, just like you. So imagine what you can do today with all the resources available to you!

JOHN THE BAPTIST TESTIFIED

John the Baptist was a powerful prophet of God, handpicked by God Himself for the singular assignment of preparing the way for the coming of Jesus Christ. John preached passionately and fearlessly to

Israel, admonishing them to repent of their sins and to turn to God. Jesus Himself said that of all persons born of women, there was none greater than John the Baptist. Now that is a powerful statement to make, especially when such a statement is made directly by God.

Yet even a prophet as powerful as John the Baptist understood his position in relation to the hierarchy of the world. He gave the following testimony about Jesus:

> *I saw the Spirit descending from heaven like a dove, and He remained upon Him {Jesus}. I did not know Him, but He who sent me to baptize with water said to me, "Upon whom you see the Spirit descending, and remaining on Him, this is He who baptizes with the Holy Spirit." And I have seen and testified that this is the Son of God.* (John 1:32-34, NKJV)

What I'm demonstrating here is that your testimony has the power to change lives for the better. Your testimony is like a light in the darkness in this world and has the ability to reveal the Grace of God to a depraved world. Jesus testified regarding the Grace of God. The apostle Paul testified about the Truth of the world, who is Jesus. Peter testified about his personal encounter with Jesus, and John the Baptist lived out his destiny by testifying about the Saviour of the world, who is Jesus. If you know Jesus, then your destiny is incomplete without you telling the world about Him. It is not too late. You can start today. The question is, "How?"

We're drilling down to the core of the matter of your testimony and how to go about releasing it to the world. And we're almost there. Before I discuss how you go about testifying, there are some important considerations to take into account. You will find them in every single case where a proper testimony is given concerning the Grace of God. These are not rules you have to follow when you testify but rather are important principles, deduced from observation, inspiration and years of engaging Christians in serious conversations surrounding this topic.

KEY OBSERVATIONS CONCERNING YOUR TESTIMONY

9

YOU MUST INDEED HAVE A GENUINE TESTIMONY IN ORDER TO TESTIFY.

I know this may sound very elementary and even comical, but it really isn't intended to be. It is very important, as a matter of fact. It appears here because it occurs much more regularly than you'd care to imagine. It is the product of succumbing to the pressures brought on by ungodly expectations imposed on you by yourself, your religious mind and your religious friends. Some may accuse Satan for manipulating them to give a false testimony, but I'll ask that we leave Satan out of this one and take full responsibility.

A genuine testimony simply means that God did something for you that you want to share with the world. This means that if one thousand dollars did not miraculously show up in your bank account, don't tell people that God put a thousand dollars in your bank account simply to have something fantastic to say since others in your group are giving their testimonies.

This also means that when you pray for something like a house and God gives you a three-bedroom home sufficient for you and your family, don't tell folks in St. Lucia while you're on vacation

that God gave you a six-bedroom five thousand square foot executive home, in an attempt to magnify God's provision in your life.
Several ungodly elements are present when you engage in dis-
pensing fake testimonies:

- You're not grateful for what God did for you.
- You don't trust that He can do more than He did.
- You don't trust His Word that promises to give you the
  desires of your heart.
- You don't trust that God knew what He was doing by
  only giving you what He gave you at the time He did.

I sense that there is room here for some confusion so let me
address it beforehand. If for godly reasons you believe that it is
God's will for your life to have a five-bedroom executive home,
then by all means go ahead and declare it until you receive it.
However make your testimony clear; that even though God
answered your prayer with a smaller house, you still believe for the
bigger one. Hence you can testify that you asked God for a house
and He supernaturally gave you one, but you believe for an even
bigger and better one because that is what your heart desires. The
only caveat here that most believers forget is that God's plan for
your life *should* trump your personal desires. Therefore God may
actually give you a much bigger house than you asked Him for
because He has already sent foster children in great need to you to
look after, but you don't know it yet. He doesn't need your or my
help in order to be God, so testify only about what He has really
done and nothing else.

Naturally your greatest testimony is your salvation. For that
unmatchable miracle of your salvation, you should be prepared to
open your mouth and testify every single day of your life. This
means that even when God hasn't given you the car, husband, wife,
children or home you desire, you still have the greatest miracle of
all to testify about, and that is your salvation. That was essentially

the crux of Peter's *3,000 souls testimony* right after Pentecost in the book of Acts.

YOUR TESTIMONY MUST *BRING* GLORY TO GOD.

What this simply means is that you cannot testify about anything that is contrary to the nature and character of God. For instance, you cannot testify that you prayed for your neighbour, who was harassing you, to die and God killed him, because that is contrary to the nature and character of God. He might actually have placed you in the path of that worrisome neighbour so that you would testify of His love and Grace to him, but instead you whined and complained and even went so far as to pray for him to die. Such an outcome is contrary to the will of God and cannot constitute a testimony.

Recently the nation of Haiti was rocked by a devastating earthquake. As I write they're just beginning to shake off the dust of depravation and suffering that settled on them from that gruesome event. Haiti is a nation known for its strong cultic heritage and practices. Once the gem of the Caribbean, it deteriorated steadily over the decades due to poor leadership and political and economic malfeasance, leaving many of the wonderful people of Haiti in desperate need of even the basics of everyday life.

When the 7.0 magnitude earthquake rocked the very foundations of Haiti and catapulted its people backwards several decades on the road of economic progress, many Christians concluded that God had judged Haiti for its cult-ridden culture. Some Christians even went as far as to testify of God's holiness, declaring erroneously that God had done to Haiti what He did to Sodom and Gomorrah.

Obviously I disagree with those Christians, because they testified falsely. For one thing, when God passes judgment on a place or a people He leaves absolutely no room for speculation as to whether

He passed judgment or not. In the case of Sodom and Gomorrah, God left a monument of His judgment by turning Lot's wife into a pillar of salt. You cannot debate whether or not that was God's judgment, because it was unique, unprecedented *and effective.*

In the days of Noah, when God had had enough of mankind's rampant and fearless sinning and decided to judge the entire world, He orchestrated a global flood that covered the highest peaks all over the world. Once again, there is no question regarding what God's intentions were during that time.

When we testify we are representing God and His kingdom. When we testify we occupy the office of heaven's ambassadors on earth. Therefore we must testify accurately, in a manner truly representative of God. Such diligence will bring glory to the name of God.

YOUR TESTIMONY MUST *GIVE* GLORY TO GOD.

Even though this point sounds very similar to the last one, the last point deals with *accurately representing* God with your testimony, while this one deals with *giving credit to God with your testimony.*

The testimony of your salvation or something else that God did in your life was really not as a *result* of your long fasting or many hours of prayer. It was instead as a result of *His Grace* and what He had already done for you when He died on the cross for your sins, your freedom, your healing and your provision. Your prayers and fasting simply enabled you to claim the blessings. This is a very important point to understand, because if you don't you risk appropriating the glory for your breakthroughs, which is both false and dangerous. It is false because you are not responsible for your breakthroughs and dangerous because God *does not* share His glory with anyone.

In Acts we find the narrative of the account of King Herod's violent death by the hand of God. The Herod in question was Herod Antipas, who was the ruler of Galilee under Rome after his father died around 4 BC. His father was the King Herod who attempted to kill the baby Jesus as recorded in Matthew.

Herod Antipas continued his father's legacy of mistreating the Jews when he took control of the territory in 4 BC. He was responsible for beheading John the Baptist and imprisoning Peter, amongst many other acts of terror against the people of Israel. But for reasons known only to God, Herod's life was spared. In fact, Jesus Christ Himself wasn't very far away when John the Baptist was beheaded. God let the murderous and tyrannical king live in spite of his evil shenanigans. However, read the Bible's account of why God finally decided to end Herod's life:

> *Now Herod had been very angry with the people of Tyre and Sidon; but they came to him with one accord, and having made Blastus the king's personal aide their friend, they asked for peace, because their country was supplied with food by the king's country. So on a set day Herod, arrayed in royal apparel, sat on his throne and gave an oration to them. And the people kept shouting, "The voice of a god and not of a man!" Then immediately an angel of the Lord struck him, because he did not give glory to God. And he was eaten by worms and died. But the word of God grew and multiplied.* (Acts 12:20-24, NKJV)

I am not suggesting that God will kill anyone who withholds the credit for their accomplishments for themselves instead of attributing them to God, but I'm saying that giving God the glory for what He has done in your life is the right thing to do.

When you think your blessings are as a result of your extended fasting and many hours of praying, you are concluding that you earned them by your own efforts, and not because God looked on you with favour. You may not like the sound of this, but the truth is that for every day you fast, someone in another part of the world is fasting for a week. I personally know people who go on forty-day fasts at least once or twice a year!

For every hour that you spend in prayer, someone in the world is praying for two or three hours. I can testify about that personally because I have been in many prayer gatherings where we prayed all night, sometimes for over eight hours nonstop. The point I'm making is that if God dispensed blessings based on how much fasting and praying we each did, some people would have everything while others would have nothing.

God does not give you testimonies because of *what* you do. He gives them to you for *who* you are; as a believer in Him, you are His.

If you are a parent or grew up in a large family, then you know that in a home there are always those who "squeak" more than others. If as a parent you respond to the one who squeaks the loudest and the most often in your home and ignore the quiet ones who give you no trouble at all, then you know you're doing something wrong. If you as an earthly parent can exercise such profound wisdom to know to give of your love, time and resources even to your quiet, undemanding kids, then how much more does God our heavenly Father, from whom all wisdom emanates?

It pleases Him that you fast and pray. It also pleases Him that you serve Him in whatever capacity you do. However, it is only by His infinite Grace that He dispenses His blessings. Otherwise most of us would never have been saved because of some of the things we were involved in prior to our encounter with the saving Grace of Jesus Christ. Thank God that His Grace operates supernaturally, and not based on the limited wisdom of humankind.

What I'm saying here is simply that you should testify in such a way that it is abundantly clear to whom you attribute your victories. It is not intended to make you change your prayer life and become lazy since you now think God does not reward you because of the length of your prayers. Your prayers are your lifeline to God. Your prayers are your access code into the throne room of God, where He eagerly awaits and rejoices in speaking with you.

Therefore pray often. God is pleased with your diligence in seeking and communicating with Him in prayer.

I have heard many church folk testify and then mention the goodness of God as though it is merely an afterthought. The temptation to attribute your successes to your prayer life and your education and your hard work and your charisma, etc., can be very strong and yet quite subtle. I have come to realize that the strength to study and work hard *and even* to pray are all because of God's Grace. In fact the Bible reminds us in many places about this:

> *Both riches and honor come from You, And You reign over all. In Your hand is power and might; In Your hand it is to make great And to give strength to all.* (I Chronicles 29:12, NKJV)

> *And you shall remember the LORD your God, for it is He who gives you power to get wealth, that He may establish His covenant which He swore to your fathers, as it is this day.* (Deuteronomy 8:18, NKJV)

Therefore as you go about testifying of the goodness and of the Grace of God in your life, be sure to give God the credit completely. The real power in your testimony lies in this knowledge. This state of humbleness as you testify is what grabs the attention of people more or less accomplished than you are.

YOUR TESTIMONY MUST NOT MAKE A MOCKERY OF GOD.

This is what I mean: you who are testifying must be a person who is humble in spirit and a person who is doing his or her best to live in holiness the way God wants you to. When you testify people should not listen to you and say something like, "If that two-faced backstabbing gossiper can testify about what God has done in his life, then I don't know what kind of God that is."

As a believer in Jesus you are His ambassador on earth and

should therefore represent Him appropriately. Your testimony ought to be like worship. It should go up to God like a sweet smelling fragrance, holy and acceptable to Him. You cannot be swearing and cursing one minute and testifying the next minute to the same people. When you do that, you make a mockery of God. You contaminate His awesome Grace with your mess in the eyes of the world and you make it harder for people to be open to receiving it. This is not a demand for you to be "perfect" before you can tell the world about God, but is simply a reminder that the God we serve is a great and mighty God, and we should therefore handle His business with reverence.

YOUR TESTIMONY IS A SEED.

I encourage you to read this section very deliberately because so far I've written on the importance of your testimony to the kingdom of God and to the ones whose lives you will affect by testifying. In this section I'm dealing with the importance of your testimonies to *you*.

So then, how can telling the world about Jesus and what He has *already* done in your life be of any *further* benefit to you? The answer is that your testimony is the catalyst for something much greater than the blessing you received from God. Your testimony is the propagator of God's agenda in the world. Your testimony is a seed and not the fruit. To begin with then, let us define a seed.

The *Oxford English Dictionary* describes a seed as "the unit of reproduction of a flowering plant, capable of developing into another such plant." You can say that a seed is the propagative portion of a plant which has the job of producing new crop given the appropriate environment or circumstances.

Note that anything designed for propagation is itself merely an instrument to be used to bring about a particular end; it is not the endpoint in itself. Therefore if your testimony is indeed a seed, then the blessing from which that testimony is derived was not in itself an endpoint, but merely an instrument to be used to propagate something else. That "something else" is the kingdom of God and God's agenda for the world.

What this means is this: just like a seed needs to be planted in order for it to realize its God-ordained purpose, which is to grow and multiply, your testimony needs to be planted in order for it to multiply and propagate the kingdom of God. Your seeds of testimony are planted when you drop them in the world, which is the field, from where the harvest of souls will come. By virtue of the fact that you are the carrier of that testimony, you are blessed.

Now that I have defined what a seed is and proposed to you that your testimony was designed simply as an instrument to propagate the kingdom of God, let me go on to establish the authority of that proposal.

1. Your testimony is the *Word of God* in action: I have discussed this previously. God's promises to save your soul, protect you and provide for you are all delineated in His Word. Your salvation and blessings are therefore the manifestations of His Word in your life.

2. The Word of God is a seed: This is abundantly obvious when you scroll through the Bible, as demonstrated by the following verses:

   • *Now the parable is this: The seed is the word of God.* (Luke 8:11)
   • *Having been born again, not of corruptible seed but incorruptible, through the word of God which lives and abides forever.* (1 Peter 1:23)
   • *The sower sows the word.* (Mark 4:14)

3. When you testify you sow the Word of God in people's hearts. The result is that people begin looking to and for God, which brings about a harvest of souls into His kingdom. Winning souls

for the kingdom of God is the most important item on God's agenda for this world. That is why the Bible declares that it is not God's wish that *even one* person should go to hell.

4. For those of you who pursue the heartbeat of God and work diligently in the field of the world to gather the harvest of souls, God's reward to you is to give you more seeds of testimony, as we see in II Corinthians: *"Now may He who supplies seed to the sower, and bread for food, **supply and multiply** the seed you have sown and increase the fruits of your righteousness"* (9:10, NKJV, emphasis added).

Every testimony in your life is an instance of a manifestation of God's blessing. Therefore as often as your seed of testimony is multiplied, the blessings in your life increase. Friend, your testimony is a reward-generating activity right here on earth.

Some Things to Note Concerning Seeds.

A seed has one purpose only, and that is to be planted so that it can multiply itself.

If your testimony is not planted, therefore, it is being wasted. One could argue that God wasted His time by blessing you with salvation and the many other blessings and testimonies He gave you, if all you do with those testimonies is nothing. A seed cannot multiply itself in its little plant-pot in the nursery. Your testimony does not help anyone if it remains in your head and never gets shared. A seed must go out into the field in order to be productive.

A seed will *never* be plentiful enough to feed you and the ones you're responsible for.

That is why one testimony of healing or a financial breakthrough or restoration of a relationship will never be sufficient to sustain you for the rest of your life. You need that single seed of testimony given to you by God to be planted so that it can multiply and keep on producing more testimonies. Your harvest of testimonies is what will keep you victorious in *all* areas of your life. A cob of corn, for instance, is barely enough for a snack for a five-year old. However, when you plant that single cob of corn and give it time to grow, it has the potential to feed your entire household all summer long. If you want more testimonies in your life, therefore, go out and testify passionately.

A seed that is not planted will perish.

This means that the testimony that God blessed you with really must be planted in the world. There are no two ways about it. I've established that previously. When you fail to plant that seed it is as though you leave your cob of corn, which was intended to be planted, out on the barn table. If you leave it there long enough it will perish or be eaten by birds or rodents. How this relates to your testimonies is this: as life continues to happen and your fair share of perils finds you, if you're not careful they may overwhelm you and choke off the victory of your testimony because of your deliberate lethargy where the things of God are concerned. You cannot be naive about this. If you do nothing you may end up with no one to blame but yourself.

FINAL THOUGHTS

You're probably still waiting to find out how you actually go about testifying. The truth is that your particular circumstance with dictate the "how." What's most important is that you remember the points you just read and apply them. If you recall, I said they are not rules but are rather information to empower you and to ensure that God gets the glory for the victories in your life and no one else. The following points may however help you get started:

Pray and ask God to give you the words to speak when you share your story.

Pray and ask God to send you the people to share your story with. Note that most of these people are already around you, so don't wait for a list to drop down from heaven!

Learn your testimony as though it was a story you wrote. This is really important, because when telling people about Jesus and what He did for you, the presentation has to be smooth and consistent. Your facts must be straight so that you don't lie or seem to be lying. Any inconsistencies or contradictions may generate the opposite effect you intended going in.

Avoid hypothesizing. This is *your* story. Speak in the first person.

Finally, remember that after you testify your job is done. You don't have the power to convict the heart of anyone you share your testimony with. That job description belongs to the Holy Spirit. You simply drop the seed, and God takes care of the rest. This means that if you see the person you testified to six months down the road and they seem like nothing has changed in them, don't beat yourself, or them, for not seeing any visible signs of change. If you give your testimony sincerely, God begins to work in the person with whom you shared your story. Therefore even though it may seem as though nothing has changed, usually that is not the case. God will send someone else in their lives to finish up the job, perhaps with their own testimony. Note that the job the other person finishes only happens because you started it. That's the way it works many times.

IT'S NOT ABOUT YOU

I've known very zealous Christians who would stop speaking with people they testified to who did not immediately ask to be led to Jesus. These overly zealous and misinformed Christians testified with deep arrogance and condemnation, pointing fingers of doom at the ones they testified to. The results were very often the same, culminating in arguments and fallouts that were sometimes irreparable. Such an aggressive and ignorant style of testifying became a liability in the kingdom of God because it drove people away from God, instead of to Him. Your testimony must be delivered with grace, love and patience.

Also, your lifestyle must corroborate the story you tell.

There are many Christians who have tasted the goodness of God many times in their lives but who, for one reason or the other, have refused to sing God's praises to their friends, neighbours and co-workers. My prayer for you is that this book encourages you to engage in the most rewarding activity in the world, which is to share the good news of Jesus Christ with the people around you. It is both your privilege and your duty but is contingent on whether or not you believe you truly love Jesus. Because if indeed you love Him you *will* tell the world about Him. If you love Him, you will do what He has called every single believer to do, which is to take the awesome news of His redemptive love to the ends of the world. It is not complicated at all.

I'm repeating some of Mathew 25 here to emphasize a very important teaching Jesus gave that is pertinent to this section of the discourse. My comments will follow. In Matthew 25 Jesus taught using the parable of the talents. He taught about a rich merchant who was going away on a long journey and distributed assignments to three of his servants. The assignments were for them to take care of his most precious possession, that being his money.

He gave a total of five talents to the first servant, and then two talents to the second servant, and finally to the third servant he gave one talent; then off he went on his journey. Upon returning home some time afterwards, the master summoned his three servants and asked for an account of the money he had left with each of them, trusting that they would each take care of the portion that had been assigned to them.

The first servant, to whom had been entrusted five talents, did the wise thing and invested the money for his master. When asked for an account, he happily produced ten talents, having invested wisely and doubling his master's money. To this servant the master said, "Well done, you good and faithful servant."

The second servant had also invested the money entrusted to him, and he too doubled the money by investing wisely. To him also the master said, "Well done, you good and faithful servant."

However, the third servant did something rather strange. This is the one to whom the master had given just one talent. He decided he wasn't going invest his master's money. When asked for an account of the money in his care, he told his master that he had been afraid to do anything with the money, so instead he dug a hole and buried the money in it. His rationale was that the money couldn't get lost in the ground and would be available for his master upon his return, because he feared his master.

Naturally this upset the rich merchant very much, who was accustomed to reaping returns on his investments. Therefore in anger he bellowed at the servant,

> *You wicked and lazy servant, you knew that I reap where I have not sown, and gather where I have not scattered seed. So you ought to have deposited my money with the bankers, and at my coming I would have received back my own with interest. So take the talent from him, and give it to him who has ten talents.*

Then he continued,

> *For to everyone who has, more will be given, and he will have abundance; but from him who does not have, even what he has will be taken away. And cast the unprofitable servant into the outer darkness. There will be weeping and gnashing of teeth.*

There are many *one talent lovers* of Jesus in the world today, and I pray that you are not one of them. However if you have been a *one talent lover* of Jesus up to now, don't feel condemned, because Jesus is giving you the opportunity right now to begin taking care of what He has entrusted you with, which is your testimony. It is not too late. You still have the opportunity to hear the Lord say to you, "Well done, you good and faithful servant."

What I'm writing about here is not my interpretation of Matthew 25:26-30. The words in that passage are the words of Jesus Himself as He taught His followers. Jesus was speaking precisely about His kingdom and the singular assignment He has given to each and every person who follows Him, to go to the ends of the earth and testify of His kingdom and what He has done in their lives.

The "ends of the earth" begins with the people around you. If you are not telling the people around you about Jesus, there is no way you can tell the people outside of your sphere of influence about Him. If you are not telling the world about Jesus, you are a *one talent lover* of Jesus, and you risk being subjected to the same treatment the lazy servant got.

Jesus' opening statement when He started this parable was *"For the kingdom of heaven is like a man traveling to a far country, who called his own servants and delivered his goods to them. And to one he gave five talents, to another two, and to another one,* **to each according to his own ability"** (Matthew 25:14-15, NKJV, emphasis added).

God knows the ability He wrote into your DNA. He is not expecting you to move to the remotest corner of Africa to become a missionary, or to build a mega Christian television network like Paul and Jan Crouch have done with TBN in the United States of America or like David and Norma Jean Mainse did with CTS in Canada.

However, this also means that the ability He has given you is enough for you to win at least one soul into His kingdom. Unfortunately available statistics indicate that only two out of every one hundred Christians will ever win a soul for Jesus. My prayer for you is that you are counted in that meagre 2 percent who are the *five and two talent lovers* of Jesus.

As I reflect on the parable of the talents I can't help but wonder if there is an explanation in there somewhere why many Christians live lives devoid of power and victory. Through casual observation I have noticed that there seems to be as much poverty amongst

Christians as there is amongst non-Christians. There also seems to be as much illness and disease, divorce and broken homes amongst Christians as there is amongst non-Christians. I don't believe it is coincidental that this is the case, when you realize that most Christians are living in blatant disobedience of Jesus' directive to go out to the world and preach His gospel. He loves your prayers. He loves your praise and worship. However, if you are not doing what He has clearly asked you to do, you are not living with power and authority in the world the way you are supposed to, because you are not representing Him the way you are supposed to. Properly representing God means you are saying what He has asked you to say and doing what He has asked you to do.

Think about it. A governor of a state or province who constantly displays drunken behaviour in public or who has a reputation for prostituting or chasing after prostitutes or who repeatedly mishandles the treasury and misrepresents the national government cannot stay in office. Likewise, a governor of a territory who fails to respond to the cries of citizens to combat crime and provide needed facilities, and also fails to adequately represent the interests of the national government, will be stripped of their office because they are not following orders. Such a person might be doomed to a future of ill-repute and powerlessness, unless they clean up their act and begin doing things the right way again.

As a Christian, you are God's representative on earth. He implanted the wisdom, power and authority of a ruler into your DNA even before you were born. If you realize that there is little or no victory or power in your life *today,* even after God has put his hand of Grace on you, the first place to look is how well you are representing Him in the world. You may very well be the reason things are not happening in your life the way you pray for them to. The good news, however, is that today is a new day!

AFTERWORD

When I first encountered the saving Grace of Jesus in my life back in 2005, I did so in an environment full of zealous Christians with great ambitions to take the good news of the love of Jesus to the world. Many of these people were so committed to God that they fasted and prayed regularly and with deep passion. They never tired of investing significant sums of money, time and other resources into ministry work and the things of God generally. I thank many of them for the wonderful example they set for me, a newly saved Christian at the time. The foundation of fervent prayers, fasting and a profound commitment to study the Word of God set the pace for my walk with God and ultimately how quickly I have become effective in ministry.

The one area that I found troubling amongst my early tutors, as I began to grow in the knowledge of God and the things that concern Him, was that some of them erroneously began attributing the successes in their lives to *their* prayer habits. Many of them would boast of how many hours they could pray for and how regularly they fasted. You almost got the feeling that they were in competition with each other, and I found that rather unsettling.

They prayed very loudly by habit, infused with great vigour and gesticulation of the hands. I find that I tend to do that as well even now, especially when I'm praying over a dire situation. The problem, however, was that my tutors just as loudly and vigorously condemned anyone who didn't pray like they did, exhibiting the same types of mannerisms. They called such persons spiritually weak.

Some of them even went as far as labelling any congregation that did not demonstrate such boisterousness in their communal prayer culture "little Holy Ghost churches," as opposed to their "prayer warrior and devil-beating churches." They had become puffed up on the power of God manifesting in their lives and actually started believing that their successes had to do with their prayer habits instead of the Grace of God.

In those early days of my conversion I felt gravely inadequate as a Christian because of some of those persons. It seemed that in their eyes God could not speak to me directly, because my knowledge of Him was still rudimentary. I felt unworthy. My opinions were brushed off as though they were those of an unruly infant. Deep down, however, I felt God guiding me on, teaching me things and revealing His Word directly to me, to the point where I knew without a shadow of a doubt that *He* had called me to ministry. I did not have to hear from anyone else concerning what He had called me to do.

I came to the joyful realization that I did not need the approval of any human being—pastor, evangelist, prophet, bishop or otherwise—in order to begin serving God. This is not to suggest that you should not listen to or seek advice from the men and women of God who have gone before you and who have ministered to and mentored you. However, Jesus Christ Himself called you to ministry, and your ultimate account is to Him alone.

When I finally walked in that knowledge, the power of God in my life multiplied and emboldened me. From a mild-mannered corporate director, I became a passionate walking testament of God's unmatchable and amazing Grace. I started communicating the message of His Grace with joy and vehemence and have never stopped to look back even once.

I want to encourage you this day that only God calls us to ministry, and when He does so He also equips us to do the work He has called us to do.

I want to leave you with this prayer, which Jesus prayed just prior to returning to heaven. My directives and power are derived from Him, and I pray that you will be struck by the same revelation that arrested my mind and has compelled and propelled me so powerfully into the ministry of Jesus Christ, who is the Saviour of the world.

JESUS' PRAYER FOR YOU

{Father,} I have manifested Your name to the men whom You have given Me out of the world. They were Yours, You gave them to Me, and they have kept Your word. Now they have known that all things which You have given Me are from You. For I have given to them the words which You have given Me; and they have received them, and have known surely that I came forth from You; and they have believed that You sent Me.

I pray for them. I do not pray for the world but for those whom You have given Me, for they are Yours. And all Mine are Yours, and Yours are Mine, and I am glorified in them. Now I am no longer in the world, but these are in the world, and I come to You. Holy Father, keep through Your name those whom You have given Me, that they may be one as We are. While I was with them in the world, I kept them in Your name. Those whom You gave Me I have kept; and none of them is lost except the son of perdition, that the Scripture might be fulfilled.

But now I come to You, and these things I speak in the world, that they may have My joy fulfilled in themselves. I have given them Your word; and the world has hated them because they are not of the world, just as I am not of the world. I do not pray that

You should take them out of the world, but that You should keep them from the evil one. They are not of the world, just as I am not of the world. Sanctify them by Your truth. Your word is truth. As You sent Me into the world, I also have sent them into the world. And for their sakes I sanctify Myself, that they also may be sanctified by the truth. (John 17:6-19, NKJV)

Amen!